Ripley's—Believe It or Not! 22nd Series

That busy Ripley
all-new collectio
raise your eyebr

If you cannot fi
Not! POCKET BOOK at your
please write to the nearest Ripley's "Believe It or
Not!" museum:

175 Jefferson Street, San Francisco,
California 94133

1500 North Wells Street, Chicago,
Illinois 60610

19 San Marco Avenue, St. Augustine,
Florida 32084

The Parkway,
Gatlinburg, Tennessee 37738

145 East Elkhorn Avenue, Estes Park,
Colorado 80517

4960 Clifton Hill, Niagara Falls, Canada

Central Promenade,
Blackpool, Lancashire, England

Ripley's—Believe It or Not! 22nd Series
is an original POCKET BOOK edition.

Other *Ripley's Believe It or Not!* titles

Published by POCKET BOOKS

22nd Series

PUBLISHED BY POCKET BOOKS PRINTED IN U.S.A.

RIPLEY'S BELIEVE IT OR NOT!® 22ND SERIES

POCKET BOOK edition published March, 1974

This original POCKET BOOK edition is printed from brand-new plates. POCKET BOOK editions are published by POCKET BOOKS, a division of Simon & Schuster, Inc., 630 Fifth Avenue, New York, N.Y. 10020. Trademarks registered in the United States and other countries.

L

PREFACE

In preparation for *Ripley's Believe It or Not! 22nd Series,* we ransacked the *Believe It or Not!* files for items befitting that number. Our search resulted in the following Believe It or Nots:

Mir Mahmud, King of Persia (1700–1725), all during his reign signed every state paper 22 times to commemorate the fact that he ascended the throne of Persia at the age of 22!

Michel Perrache, a French sculptor and author (1680–1750), produced 22 books, 22 statues of the Apostles, and 22 children in a period of 22 years!

A reader named George X. Athanapulos of Los Angeles wrote to call attention to his full middle name which was XIXI. He explained that he had married two wives in succession, each of whom was the 11th child of her parents. He commemorated it by the curious arrangement of the Roman numerals adding to 22!

Bald Niccolo Calvo of Torino, Italy (1811–1892), boasted that for 22 generations (over 400 years) each of his male ancestors was bald. When he was asked how he could be sure of such a thing, he stated that his earliest bald forebear took the name Calvo, meaning bald, as his surname, but that he enjoined his descendants to change the family name to Peloso (hairy) the first time the streak was broken!

Old No. 22 was the name proudly applied to himself by François Duvalier, the President of Haiti, who was elected on September 22, 1957, and inaugurated October 22, 1957. He considered 22 his magic number identifiable with himself. All during his reign he endeavored to mark the day with parades and great state decisions. He was content to die on April 21, 1971, so that his son Jean-Claude could inherit the magic of the number by being sworn into the Presidency on the 22nd of the month!

The thrust of this laborious effort is that *Believe It or Not!* is the most universal compilation of strange facts. No effort is ever spared to make every *Believe It or Not!* statement factual and foolproof. The most impartial perusal will bear out this opinion. In researching the material, we go to great lengths to obtain authentic illustrations. This is so well known that we are often beseeched by relatives to share with them a portrait of a long-lost ancestor. The illustrations are the work of our colleague, the esteemed cartoonist Paul Frehm, while the undersigned evinces pride in his role as Researcher for the most readable feature.

—Norbert Pearlroth
Research Director
BELIEVE IT OR NOT!

A **HUGE SYCAMORE** 300 YEARS OLD SO INTRIGUED MRS. FLORENCE SNYDER of Los Angeles, Calif., THAT SHE BOUGHT THE LAND AROUND IT AND **DESIGNED A HOUSE TO MATCH THE TREE** *THE WALLS ARE STAINED THE COLOR OF THE SYCAMORE'S BARK, AND THE ROOF RESEMBLES THE TREE'S FOLIAGE*

THE INHABITED BRIDGE
Canterbury, England

THE TALL BRIDGE ERECTED OVER THE RIVER STOUR IN 1270 SO A SETTLEMENT OF GREY FRIARS COULD REACH THEIR ISLAND PROPERTY HAS BEEN CONVERTED TO A HOME AND IS STILL OCCUPIED **691 YEARS LATER**

KING
RICHARD THE LIONHEART

NEEDING MONEY FOR HIS CRUSADE GRANTED SCOTLAND ITS INDEPENDENCE *FOR A PRICE AMOUNTING TO $3,230*

7

STRATTON'S FOLLY A TOWER IN Little Berkhamstead, England, 130 FEET HIGH WAS BUILT BY AN AMATEUR ASTRONOMER —BUT HE NEVER USED IT BECAUSE HE SUFFERED FROM *A FEAR OF HIGH PLACES*

MRS. **JOE PRESCIADO** of Santa Catalina Island, Calif., SWAM ACROSS AVALON BAY FROM ABALONE POINT TO SUGAR LOAF *AT THE AGE OF 90!*

A *BABY CAMEL* WHEN IT TIRES *IS CARRIED ON THE BACK OF ITS MOTHER*

ROCK WITH THE NATURAL OUTLINE OF A BUTTERFLY

BEDOUIN HUNTERS CREEP UP ON GAME BY *DISGUISING THEMSELVES AS BIRDS*

Stone Hearts WERE PLACED BY BRITONS 2,000 YEARS AGO *IN THE GRAVES OF MISERS*

AN **ARCHWAY** WAS CREATED IN THE ABBEY OF YORK, (England) SOLELY TO PROVIDE KING HENRY VII WITH *A SHORTCUT IN HIS JOURNEY TO SCOTLAND* (1497) THE MONARCH TOOK A DIFFERENT ROUTE AND NEVER USED IT

OPTICAL ILLUSION 2 PERFECT SQUARES

2-HEADED TURTLE FOUND NEAR POWELL, MISS.

9

A **RAILROAD** in Stephansort, Papua, *IS POWERED BY OXEN*

Henrietta LONDON'S FAMOUS COCKATOO *LAID AN EGG FOR THE FIRST TIME AT THE AGE OF 102*

THE CHIMNEYS NATURAL ROCK FORMATION near Staunton, Va.

KING PYA SRI WORAWENG of Siam 1629 -1656

BECAUSE HIS YOUNG DAUGHTER HAD DIED

KILLED 3,000 OF HIS OWN SUBJECTS

THE ROYAL CHAPEL in Laeken, Belgium, BUILT BY KING LEOPOLD II IN 1892 IS MADE ENTIRELY OF GLASS AND IRON —TO RESEMBLE THE ROYAL GREENHOUSES WHICH SURROUND IT

THE MARKER OVER THE GRAVE OF SARA WINN WHO DIED SEPT. 3, 1770 AT THE AGE OF 2 *WAS HER WOODEN CRADLE* Midway, Ga.

THE CHIEFS OF THE **MACLEOD CLAN** PROVED THEIR WORTHINESS FOR **500 YEARS** BY EMPTYING IN ONE BREATH *The Rory Mor Drinking Horn* —A DRAUGHT OF 2 QUARTS

THE POINTED HUT near Apt, France, **18** FEET HIGH AND WITH WALLS **3** FEET THICK *WAS BUILT WITHOUT MORTAR OF ANY KIND* -YET IT HAS ENDURED FOR **3000 YEARS**

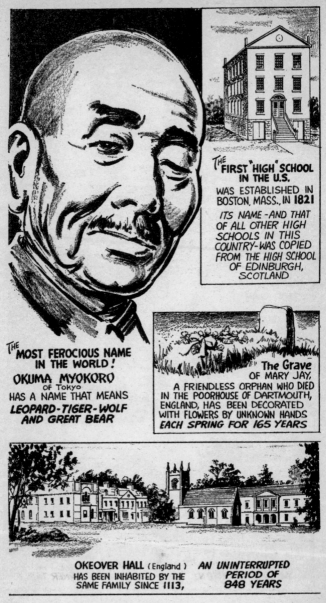

THE FIRST "HIGH" SCHOOL IN THE U.S. WAS ESTABLISHED IN BOSTON, MASS., IN 1821

ITS NAME - AND THAT OF ALL OTHER HIGH SCHOOLS IN THIS COUNTRY - WAS COPIED FROM THE HIGH SCHOOL OF EDINBURGH, SCOTLAND

THE MOST FEROCIOUS NAME IN THE WORLD!
OKUMA MYOKORO OF Tokyo
HAS A NAME THAT MEANS LEOPARD-TIGER-WOLF AND GREAT BEAR

The Grave OF MARY JAY, A FRIENDLESS ORPHAN WHO DIED IN THE POORHOUSE OF DARTMOUTH, ENGLAND, HAS BEEN DECORATED WITH FLOWERS BY UNKNOWN HANDS EACH SPRING FOR 165 YEARS

OKEOVER HALL (England) HAS BEEN INHABITED BY THE SAME FAMILY SINCE 1113, AN UNINTERRUPTED PERIOD OF 848 YEARS

THE GREATEST SNOWFALL IN THE HISTORY OF THE U.S. WAS RECORDED WEST of Squaw Valley, Calif., IN THE WINTER OF 1906-7 - *A FALL OF 73' 8"*

THE MOST AMAZING JURIST IN ALL HISTORY Prince Shotoku (574-622) JURIST SON OF JAPANESE EMPEROR YOMEI *COULD LISTEN TO EVIDENCE IN 10 LAWSUITS SIMULTANEOUSLY !*

THE REV. GEORGE F. TYLER of Sterling, Pa. WAS THE FATHER OF 4 MINISTERS *- 3 METHODIST AND ONE EPISCOPALIAN*

THE COFFIN OF ANTHONY BRAGGE of Charmouth, England, AT HIS OWN REQUEST WAS MADE *FROM HIS DINNER TABLE*

13

A **WOODEN BRIDGE** OVER THE KENTUCKY RIVER, in Jessamine County, Ky., 270 FEET LONG, WAS BUILT UPRIVER IN 1838 BY LEWIS B. WERNWAG, FLOATED DOWN IN SECTIONS ON A RAFT, AND HAD BEEN PLANNED SO EXACTLY THAT IT WAS PUT TOGETHER *WITHOUT THE USE OF A HAMMER*

Marcellus **PIUS** AN INDIAN of the Santa Clara Mission, Calif., DIED IN 1875 AT THE AGE OF 130, *HAVING OUTLIVED 5 WIVES*

THE **PRAYER WALL of LEH** in Ladakh, Kashmir, A WALL 2,300 FEET LONG, BUILT BY KING SENGE OF HOLLOW BRICKS— **EACH OF WHICH CONTAINS A PRAYER FOR HIS MOTHER**— *PILGRIMS WALK AROUND THE WALL IN SILENCE IN THE BELIEF THAT EACH STEP SERVES AS A PRAYER FOR THE QUEEN*

A HUSBAND
IN THE KENIAGUI TRIBE, in Gambia, Africa, ALWAYS LIVES ALONE
-ACROSS THE STREET FROM THE HOME OF HIS WIFE

THE ONLY GUILLOTINE
EVER ERECTED ON WHAT IS NOW UNITED STATES SOIL WAS BUILT IN THE PLACE D'ARMES in New Orleans, La., IN 1793
AND AVERAGED ONE EXECUTION A WEEK DURING THE FRENCH REVOLUTION'S REIGN OF TERROR

ABDALLAH IBN MALIK
CHIEF OF POLICE OF BAGHDAD, TO ATONE FOR AN ACT OF TREASON IN 785 WALKED ALL THE WAY TO MECCA AND BACK, A PILGRIMAGE OF 2,500 MILES—
BUT HE MADE THE ENTIRE JOURNEY ON QUILTS SPREAD ON THE DESERT SANDS BY AN ARMY OF SLAVES!

WROTTESLEY MANOR (-England)
HAS BEEN INHABITED BY THE SAME FAMILY FOR **798** YEARS

THE Earl of Angus (1489-1557) AS A BOY FELL IN LOVE WITH QUEEN MARGARET of Scotland, SISTER OF KING HENRY VIII, **AND WHEN HE GREW UP MARRIED 3 MARGARETS IN SUCCESSION** *- HIS SECOND WIFE BEING QUEEN MARGARET HERSELF, WHO HAD BECOME A WIDOW IN 1513*

THE Arch of Triumph in Barcelona, Spain, WAS ORIGINALLY CONSTRUCTED AS *THE ENTRANCE GATE TO THE BARCELONA FAIR IN 1888*

MEN OF ANGORAM, New Guinea, WEAR 2 SETS OF WHISKERS - IN ADDITION TO THE NORMAL BEARD A MAN WEARS A NECKLACE CONSISTING OF THE WHISKERS OF HIS DEPARTED FATHER

THE WELL of PUTTUR on the Jaffna Peninsula, 180 FEET DEEP, IS SALTY FROM 80 FEET DOWN *- BUT ITS UPPER LEVEL IS SO FRESH THAT IT IS USED TO IRRIGATE THE SURROUNDING COUNTRYSIDE* Ceylon

THE MOJAVE GROUND SQUIRREL
of the California desert area
*SLEEPS 8 MONTHS
OF EACH YEAR*

DO NOT DISTURB

WOOL HALL
in Lavenham, England,
DEMOLISHED IN 1913,
WAS REBUILT ON ITS ORIGINAL
SITE FROM ITS ORIGINAL
BUILDING MATERIALS
*-WHICH HAD BEEN STORED
IN LONDON FOR 2 YEARS*

THE LOOKOUT
Santa Cruz Island, Calif.,
NATURAL STONE FORMATION

A **HUGE CAULDRON** IN THE
Church of Frensham, England,
HAS NOT BEEN DISTURBED
FOR CENTURIES
*BECAUSE IT IS BELIEVED
TO HAVE ONCE BEEN
THE PROPERTY OF
"THE LITTLE PEOPLE"*

The **PEOPLE** WHO SPEAK IN CODE !
THE MUKANKALAS
of Angola, Portuguese Africa,
HAVE A LANGUAGE CONSISTING ONLY
OF A SINGLE CONSONANT-"KH"
*THEY COMMUNICATE AS BY MORSE CODE BY
MERELY REPEATING THE SOUND "KH"
AT VARYING SPEEDS AND
AT DIFFERENT INTERVALS*

17

THE HEN THAT GIVES MILK

IT PRODUCES BOTH EGGS—AND MILK

Owned by
SHEIKH UMAR
Gujar Khan,
Pakistan

THE FIRST SOUND-PROOF WALLS
WERE IN A HOME DESIGNED IN 1851 FOR THE GREAT LONDON EXHIBITION
BY PRINCE ALBERT

THE HOUSE WAS MOVED TO KENSINGTON PARK, WHERE IT STILL SERVES AS A RESIDENCE FOR THE PARK SUPERINTENDENT

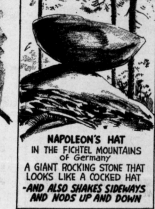

KING SAHALE SELASSIE
of Shoa, Ethiopia,
CELEBRATED EACH NEW YEAR'S
BY PERSONALLY PAYING THE DEBTS OF EVERY PAUPER IN HIS KINGDOM

NAPOLEON'S HAT
IN THE FICHTEL MOUNTAINS
of Germany
A GIANT ROCKING STONE THAT LOOKS LIKE A COCKED HAT
—AND ALSO SHAKES SIDEWAYS AND NODS UP AND DOWN

THE SHIVA TEMPLE of Utterkashi, India, WAS BUILT TO ENSHRINE AN ANCIENT PILLAR OF METAL 26 FEET HIGH **BECAUSE IT HAS MYSTERIOUSLY REMAINED FREE OF RUST** *FOR 2,400 YEARS*

JUDGE JOHN G. WILKIN (1818-1889) of Middletown, N.Y., WHO PRACTICED LAW FOR 36 YEARS, WAS SO SUSPICIOUS OF WOMEN THAT HE NEVER REPRESENTED ONE IN COURT *AND REFUSED TO PARTICIPATE IN ANY TRANSACTION IN WHICH A WOMAN WAS INVOLVED*

ELBURS, A TOWN ON THE SLOPE of Mount Elburs, in Iran, IS SO CONSTRUCTED THAT THE ROOFS OF HOUSES ON ONE LEVEL *SERVE AS THE STREET FOR THE NEXT HIGHER ROW OF HOMES*

104 TOMATOES GROWING ON ONE BUSH

AN **EGG**
OPENED BY
JUDY FORINO
CONTAINED A DIME
Mechanicville, N.Y.

CATALPA TREE
GROWING OUT OF A
SECOND-STORY WINDOW SILL
Winchester, Va.

THE **FIRST $1,000,000 DEAL IN HISTORY**
ARON THE TYRANT IN BUYING THE
THRONE OF MOLDAVIA (now Rumania)
FROM THE SULTAN OF TURKEY IN 1591
CONSUMMATED THE FIRST TRANSACTION INVOLVING 1,000,000 THALERS

THE **ANCIENT KEYS**
STILL USED BY THE CAVE
DWELLERS
of Medenine,
Tunisia,
AFTER 3,000
YEARS, ARE
1 FOOT,
4 INCHES
LONG AND
MADE OF
WOOD
-YET EACH KEY OPENS ONLY ONE LOCK

A **DUST RAG**
TOSSED
ON A LADDER
DRAPED
ITSELF INTO
THE PROFILE
OF A MAN WEARING A HAT

THE ROLLING STONE of NANKING
China
A BOULDER SO FINELY BALANCED
ON A HILLTOP THAT IT IS ROLLED
FROM SIDE TO SIDE BY THE WIND
*-YET IT NEVER ROLLS
OVER THE EDGE*

**LEATHER
WINE BOTTLES**
in medieval times
*WERE SHAPED LIKE
THE ANIMALS FROM
WHOSE PELTS THE
BOTTLES WERE MADE*

**FRANCIS
BROADLEY**
of
Brighouse,
England,

**AT THE
AGE OF
18
IN 1844
WALKED
50
MILES IN
12
CONSECUTIVE
HOURS
TO WIN
A WAGER
OF
$4.85**

**ST. ANDREW'S
CHURCH** in Kingsbury, England,
WAS CONSTRUCTED FROM THE DEBRIS
OF THE ORIGINAL CHURCH
*-WHICH STOOD 120 MILES AWAY
IN LONDON*

THE MONUMENT in Columbia, S.C., HONORING SOLDIERS OF THE PALMETTO STATE KILLED IN THE MEXICAN WAR *IS A BRONZE PALMETTO TREE*

MARRIED WOMEN in Laos MUST ALWAYS WEAR THEIR HAIR IN A BUN -*IN THE BELIEF IT WILL MAKE THEM LESS ATTRACTIVE TO OTHER MEN*

THE **WOMAN** WHO WALKED SITTING DOWN MARGARET FINCH A GYPSY QUEEN of Norwood, England, WHO DIED IN 1740 AT THE AGE OF 108

HAD SQUATTED ON THE GROUND FOR SO MANY YEARS THAT SHE COULD WALK ONLY IN A SITTING POSITION *WITH HER CHIN AS LOW AS HER KNEES*

"Lutembe" A SACRED CROCODILE in Lake Victoria, Nyanza, Africa, BECAME SO TAME THAT IT WOULD *COME ASHORE WHEN CALLED*

22

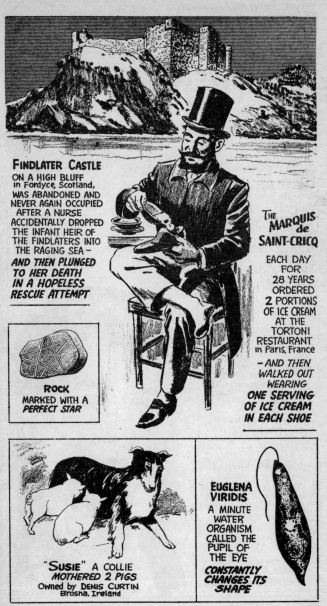

FINDLATER CASTLE
ON A HIGH BLUFF in Fordyce, Scotland, WAS ABANDONED AND NEVER AGAIN OCCUPIED AFTER A NURSE ACCIDENTALLY DROPPED THE INFANT HEIR OF THE FINDLATERS INTO THE RAGING SEA – *AND THEN PLUNGED TO HER DEATH IN A HOPELESS RESCUE ATTEMPT*

ROCK
MARKED WITH A *PERFECT STAR*

THE MARQUIS de SAINT-CRICQ
EACH DAY FOR 28 YEARS ORDERED **2** PORTIONS OF ICE CREAM AT THE TORTONI RESTAURANT in Paris, France –*AND THEN WALKED OUT WEARING* ***ONE SERVING OF ICE CREAM IN EACH SHOE***

"SUSIE" A COLLIE *MOTHERED 2 PIGS* Owned by DENIS CURTIN Brosna, Ireland

EUGLENA VIRIDIS A MINUTE WATER ORGANISM CALLED THE PUPIL OF THE EYE *CONSTANTLY CHANGES ITS SHAPE*

THE MOST POMPOUS MAN IN THE WORLD!

The 8TH Earl of ABERCORN (1712-1789) WAS SO DIGNIFIED THAT DURING A COACH TRIP THROUGH EUROPE THAT TOOK 2 YEARS *HE NEVER ONCE RELAXED ENOUGH TO LET HIS BACK TOUCH THE CUSHION BEHIND HIM*

THE SHIFTING BLOCKS OPTICAL ILLUSION

"Tom" A CAT OWNED BY MRS. NICK RADAKOVICH FOUND ITS WAY HOME From Lake Isabel, Colo., to Pueblo *TRAVELING 55 MILES IN 12 DAYS*

JOHN W. VAN CLEVE
(1801-1858)
THE FIRST BOY BORN IN the city of Dayton, Ohio, ENTERED OHIO UNIVERSITY AT THE AGE OF 16, *TAUGHT LATIN AT THE UNIVERSITY WHEN HE WAS 17, AND AT 18, WHILE STILL AN UNDERGRADUATE,* **WAS A PROFESSOR OF LATIN AND GREEK**

THE TOWER in Portobello, Scotland, **WAS BUILT FROM THE DEBRIS OF 3 FAMED STRUCTURES** -THE CROSS OF EDINBURGH, THE CATHEDRAL OF ST. ANDREWS AND OLD EDINBURGH COLLEGE

GENERAL WILLIAM MACKINTOSH (1662-1743) IMPRISONED 24 YEARS IN EDINBURGH CASTLE FOR HIS PART IN THE JACOBITE REBELLION OF 1715 *EXTRACTED ONE OF HIS OWN TEETH ON THE EVE OF HIS DEATH TO SCRATCH ON THE WALL OF HIS CELL* "Long live King James VIII !"

Calf WITH 6 LEGS Owned by PETER CHRIST Factoryville, Pa.

AN ASH TREE GREW ON THE VESTRY ROOF OF THE CHURCH OF ASKRIGG, ENGLAND, FOR 150 YEARS

ELIZABETH PERCY (1667-1722)
ENGLAND'S RICHEST HEIRESS
WAS WIDOWED TWICE BEFORE SHE WAS 15 YEARS OF AGE—
SHE LIVED HAPPILY WITH HER THIRD HUSBAND FOR **40** YEARS

DEVIL'S TABLE
near Gräfenberg, Germany,
NATURAL STONE FORMATION

THE **CATHEDRAL of FERRARA** in Italy
HAS A ROW OF SHOPS BUILT INTO THE SOUTH SIDE OF THE EDIFICE

A **STONE TABLET**
FOUND IN A WOMAN'S GRAVE IN AN ANCIENT ROMAN CEMETERY IN BALDOCK, ENGLAND, IS INSCRIBED:
"Tacita, or by whatever name she is called now, is hereby cursed"

THE **GRAVE** of **3** SAILORS WHO PERISHED IN THE SHIPWRECK OF THE SCHOONER "MINNA" at Zingst, Germany, in April, 1912
IS DECORATED WITH THE VESSEL'S ANCHOR, CHAIN AND WHEEL

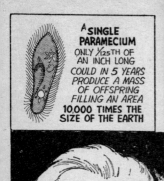

A SINGLE PARAMECIUM ONLY 1/125TH OF AN INCH LONG COULD IN 5 YEARS PRODUCE A MASS OF OFFSPRING FILLING AN AREA **10,000 TIMES THE SIZE OF THE EARTH**

JAMES T. BELK (1765-1876) of Charlotte, N.C., WHO WITNESSED THE CELEBRATION OF THE ORIGINAL INDEPENDENCE DAY AS A BOY OF 11, *LIVED TO PARTICIPATE IN THE CENTENARY CELEBRATION*

JOSEPH DRINKWATER (1709-1784) of Yarmouth, Maine, WAS THE FATHER OF **9 SEA CAPTAINS** *AND MARRIED HIS DAUGHTER TO A 10TH CAPTAIN*

THE **RABBITS** THAT ARE **VENTRILOQUISTS**

Pikas found in the Canadian Rockies *"THROW" THEIR SHRILL WHISTLE TO CONFUSE PREYING EAGLES*

27

THE HOUSES THAT FLOAT ON PAPER
The Mpologoma River, Africa

NATIVES BUILD THEIR HUTS ON PLATFORMS MADE BY STAMPING SHEETS OF PAPYRUS *INTO GIANT PAPER RAFTS*

A SINGLE GIRL
in the Montafon Valley in Vorarlberg, Austria,

ADVERTISES THAT SHE IS SEEKING A HUSBAND BY *WEARING A MINIATURE GOLD CROWN*

THE FAÇADE OF THE CHURCH OF THE CONCEPTION
Lisbon, Portugal,

WAS FORMERLY THE SIDE ENTRANCE OF A HOSPITAL WHICH WAS DESTROYED BY AN EARTHQUAKE IN 1755 *THE WALL STOOD AS A RUIN FOR 100 YEARS - AFTER WHICH THE CHURCH WAS BUILT BEHIND IT*

SHELL OF A SEA SCORPION (Eurypterus fischeri) FOUND PRESERVED 300,000,000 YEARS AFTER ITS EXTINCTION

PRISONER'S TREE
of Nalgee, Australia—
AN OLD BOTTLE TREE WITH A HOLLOW
TRUNK AND A DOOR WAS LONG USED
AS A LOCK-UP FOR CULPRITS

William S. Gould
of Scranton, Pa.,
WAS ELECTED SECRETARY
OF HIS ELKS LODGE
FOR 67 CONSECUTIVE YEARS

THE GIANT ANTHILLS of Africa
OFTEN **20 FEET HIGH AND
15 FEET IN DIAMETER**
ARE MADE OF CLAY AND MIXED
*WITH A STRANGE CEMENT
THAT MAKES THEM WATERPROOF*

A **HOUSE** in Arroyo Seco, Calif,
CONSTRUCTED OF
OLD TELEPHONE POLES

THE FRENCH HOSPITAL
in Finsbury, London, England,
WAS BUILT ON A SITE LEASED
IN 1716 FOR A PERIOD OF **990 YEARS**
*- AT AN ANNUAL RENTAL
OF ONE PEPPERCORN*

YE DICK WHITTINGTON
THE OLDEST LICENSED TAVERN
in London, England,
*HAS BEEN SERVING PATRONS
FOR 500 YEARS*

FRANCIS BURT
THE FIRST GOVERNOR
of Nebraska Territory
TOOK HIS OATH OF OFFICE
ON OCTOBER 16, 1854
-AND DIED 2 DAYS LATER

A **CRIMINAL**
WHO INJURED
A WOMAN
IN FRANCE
- UNDER THE
OLD CODE
OF LAWS-
*WAS
REQUIRED
TO WEAR
FEMININE
CLOTHING
DURING HIS
ENTIRE
TERM OF
IMPRISONMENT*

THE WORLD'S FIRST SAVINGS BANK WAS FOUNDED BY A SCOTSMAN

The Savings and Friendly Society, THE FIRST REAL SAVINGS INSTITUTION, WAS CREATED IN 1810 BY THE REV. HENRY DUNCAN IN RUTHWELL VILLAGE, DUMFRIESSHIRE, SCOTLAND

THE COTTAGE IN WHICH THE BANK WAS LOCATED IS STILL STANDING 151 YEARS LATER

from an old print

SIR JOHN BARNARD (1685-1764) LORD MAYOR OF LONDON AND MEMBER OF THE BRITISH PARLIAMENT, WAS DESCRIBED BY ENGLAND'S PRIME MINISTER, SIR ROBERT WALPOLE, *AS THE ONLY INCORRUPTIBLE MEMBER OF PARLIAMENT FOR A PERIOD OF 39 YEARS*

PALO ALTO (Spanish for a Tall Tree) AFTER WHICH THE CITY OF PALO ALTO WAS NAMED *IS CALIFORNIA'S OLDEST LIVING LANDMARK*

IT WAS A TWIN TREE WHEN IT WAS FIRST SIGHTED IN 1769 – BUT ONE TRUNK BLEW DOWN YEARS AGO IN A STORM

Calf WITH 6 LEGS Owned by GARY BEEMAN, East Hartland, Conn.

31

MOZART'S GRAVE in Vienna
IS EMPTY
THE FAMED COMPOSER WAS BURIED IN A PAUPERS' CEMETERY AND HIS BODY WAS NEVER FOUND

W.A. MOZART 1756-1

NAMGYAL
CHIEF LAMA of the Lamasery of Tikse, in Ladakh, Kashmir,
FOR THE FIRST **20** YEARS OF HIS LIFE,
SUDDENLY VANISHED FROM THE LAMASERY
-AND BECAME THE NOTORIOUS LEADER OF A BAND OF HIGHWAYMEN

THE **TEMPLE of Thong-Warang** in Tashiding, Sikkim, in the Himalayas,
IS CONSIDERED SO SACRED THAT BUDDHISTS BELIEVE
THE MERE SIGHT OF IT CLEANSES A PILGRIM OF ALL SINS

A **CHEST** in the Church of Stoke d'Abernon, England,
WAS USED **700** YEARS AGO TO
COLLECT MONEY FOR THE CRUSADES

WINESTEAD AN ENGLISH MANOR AND ESTATE, WAS BOUGHT BY SIR WILLIAM HILTON IN 1288 *FOR A SINGLE RED ROSE*

BUST OF **JOSEPH HAYDN** in the Art Museum of Vienna UTILIZES THE AUSTRIAN COMPOSER'S *OWN HAIR AND PART OF HIS OWN CLOTHING*

THE **PERIPATUS** — A TYPE OF WORM — HAS NOT CHANGED IN 320,000,000 YEARS

Charles James Fox (1749-1806) ONE OF BRITAIN'S MOST CELEBRATED STATESMEN *LOST MORE THAN $1,000,000 AT CARDS BEFORE HE WAS 21 YEARS OF AGE*

26 ROCKS FOUND ON LUMMI ISLAND, WASH., IN A SINGLE DAY — EACH BEARS A DIFFERENT LETTER AND TOGETHER THEY COMPRISE THE ENTIRE ALPHABET

FAIRYLAND CAVERN
near Castleton, England,
CONTAINS A 40-FOOT WATERFALL

LADISLAS POSTHUMUS
WHO WAS BORN AFTER THE
DEATH OF HIS FATHER,
WAS CROWNED
KING OF HUNGARY
AT THE AGE OF 3 MONTHS
-SEATED ON THE THRONE
ON HIS MOTHER'S LAP
May 15, 1440

THE LECTERN in
THE CHURCH OF NOTRE DAME
in Bulat, France,
IS IN THE
FORM OF A
LIFE-SIZE
STATUE OF A
MAN HOLDING
ALOFT THE TOP
OF A PULPIT-

IT WAS
DONATED BY
A MAN WHO
WISHED TO
COMMEMORATE
THE FACT THAT

**HE ALWAYS
HELD THE
STAND FROM
WHICH THE
PASTOR READ
HIS SERMONS**

THE BOATS THAT LOOKED LIKE
HUGE FOOTBALLS
MEDIEVAL JAPANESE BOATS
MADE OF CAMPHOR WOOD
AND PROPELLED BY WHEELS
TURNED BY HUMAN HANDS

34

THE SAAS VALLEY
in Switzerland
AFTER A DISASTROUS FLOOD IN 1680, FOR A PERIOD OF **40** YEARS BANNED
CARD PLAYING, DANCING, DRINKING AND PARTIES -
THE VALLEY'S NEXT FLOOD WAS IN 1772

The **YOUNGEST FATHER**
Richard Michael FATHER
WAS BORN ON FATHER'S DAY
Albany, N.Y.

Sunflower
22 INCHES IN DIAMETER
WITH **LEAVES 19** INCHES LONG
Grown by DONALD MUNRO Montague, Prince Edward Island, Canada

AUGUSTE **RODIN**
1840-1917
THE GREATEST FRENCH SCULPTOR, IN HIS YOUTH WAS REJECTED 3 TIMES BY THE ÉCOLE DES BEAUX ARTS, A FAMOUS ART SCHOOL, *FOR LACK OF TALENT*

THE SAME EARRINGS
WERE WORN BY QUEEN CATHERINE
of Braganza (1638-1705)
THE WIFE OF KING CHARLES II of England
EVERY DAY FOR 57 YEARS

THE **CASTLE** THAT WAS BUILT
IN A SINGLE NIGHT!
TAIKO THE GREAT,
A JAPANESE WAR LORD
SENT TO QUELL THE
REBELLIOUS OWNER
of Odawara Castle,
OVERAWED THE REBEL
BY BUILDING OVERNIGHT
A REALISTIC CASTLE
BIGGER THAN ODAWARA
-*OUT OF CARDBOARD!*

THE **ANCIENT
CASTLE of DUDLEY** (England) BUILT IN 1320
IS STILL IN USE -*BUT AS THE TOWN ZOO*

THE MEMORIAL TO A HORSE

A MONUMENT IN A CITY PARK IN Sachsenhausen, Germany, HONORS THE MOUNT THAT SAVED THE LIFE OF CONSUL VON BETHMANN IN A BATTLE AGAINST THE SOLDIERS OF NAPOLEON

THE MAUGARNI DOOR LEADING TO THE Chapel of St. Joseph, in the Cathedral of Meaux, France, *BEARS THE NAME OF A MURDERER* — THE CHURCH WAS UPHELD BY THE COURTS IN PROTESTING THE HOLDING OF EXECUTIONS OUTSIDE ITS CHAPEL, AND AS A REMINDER TO CIVIL AUTHORITIES **NAMED THE DOOR FOR THE LAST MURDERER SO EXECUTED**

E. TYRRELL SMITH MANAGER OF THE Cremorne Gardens amusement park in London, England, SOLELY TO GIVE THE APPEARANCE OF AFFLUENCE, ALWAYS CARRIED A BORROWED 1,000-POUND BANKNOTE FOR **9** YEARS -PAYING A MONEY LENDER $4.94 A DAY IN INTEREST

A Blue Bowl IN WHICH KING WILLIAM III of England WAS CHRISTENED HAS BEEN USED FOR THE BAPTISM OF EVERY CHILD BORN in Basset Down Manor, England, IN THE *PAST 273 YEARS*

THE WINDOWLESS ROUND HOUSES of Bari, Italy, WHICH ARE COOL EVEN ON THE HOTTEST DAYS, WERE BUILT OF STONES PILED ONE ATOP ANOTHER *WITHOUT MORTAR OF ANY KIND*

THOMAS SPRING
1456-1523

A WEALTHY MERCHANT of London, England, BOUGHT FROM KING HENRY VII IN 1508 A GENERAL PARDON THAT WOULD EXEMPT HIM FROM PUNISHMENT *FOR MURDER, FELONIES, REBELLION, CONTEMPT, CORRUPTION AND DECEPTION !*

THE LEANING HOUSES of BENWICK England STAND ON SHIFTING SOIL —YET THEY ARE FULLY INHABITED

PLEASE WALK ON THE GRASS

SIGN IN TORONTO, ONT., PARKS

"BICYCLE WINDOW" in the Church of Stoke Poges, England, FEATURING A FIGURE ASTRIDE AN ANCIENT WHEELED HOBBYHORSE WAS MADE BY PIECING TOGETHER FRAGMENTS OF STAINED GLASS FROM MANY BROKEN CHURCH WINDOWS

Emperor ALEXANDER I of Russia ONCE SUFFERED A HEADACHE THAT COST $10,000,000!

THE COURT DOCTOR ORDERED CANDLES SO THE EMPEROR COULD INHALE THEIR SMOKE-- BUT 91 YEARS LATER **4,000,000** TAPERS WERE FOUND IN THE PALACE--BECAUSE NO ONE HAD CANCELLED THE **DAILY DELIVERY** OF CANDLES!

MONKS of the Zhamspa Sect Tibet

ARE FORBIDDEN

TO EAT VEGETABLES OR FISH-
TO USE FIRE OR SALT-
TO SMOKE - SING - DANCE
OR PLAY A MUSICAL INSTRUMENT-
TO SLEEP IN A BED OR SIT IN A CHAIR!

LORD ROKEBY
(1713-1800)
WAS THE ONLY BEARDED NOBLEMAN OF HIS TIME IN *ALL GREAT BRITAIN AND IRELAND*

THE **TOWER** OF
The Cathedral of St. Sauveur
IN BRUGES, BELGIUM,
WAS UNDER CONSTRUCTION *FOR 774 YEARS* (1116~1890)

DON LUIS ANTONIO de BORBON
1724-1785
WAS A CARDINAL AND ARCHBISHOP of Toledo, Spain, *AT THE AGE OF 8 YEARS*

100 EARS OF CORN RANGING FROM 2" TO 6" IN LENGTH *GROWING OUT OF THE TASSEL OF A SINGLE STALK OF CORN*

A **Potato** SHAPED LIKE A *HEART*

THE ROYAL GUARD of SWEDEN ORDERED TO WEAR MUSTACHES WITHOUT DELAY AFTER THE CORONATION OF KING KARL JOHANN XIV IN 1818, *WHILE WAITING FOR REAL MUSTACHES TO GROW IN HAD TO PAINT FACSIMILES ON THEIR UPPER LIPS*

A DOUBLE STAIRWAY in the Castle of Graz, Austria, CONSTRUCTED IN 1490 BY EMPEROR FREDERICK III *SO PERSONS LEAVING WOULD NOT SEE THOSE ARRIVING*

THE IRON GATE of Panmure, Scotland, THROUGH WHICH THE LAST EARL OF PANMURE FLED AFTER THE COLLAPSE OF THE JACOBITE UPRISING IN 1715 *HAS REMAINED LOCKED FOR 246 YEARS*

The Grave of **LAURENCE STERNE** 1713 - 1768 *THE ENGLISH HUMORIST* in St. George's Cemetery, London, England, *IS IDENTIFIED BY 2 FULL-SIZED TOMBSTONES*

M.W. EARL TELLER IN A BANK in Ottawa, Ont., WAS ASKED TO CASH A CHECK WHICH HE RECOGNIZED AS A FORGERY - *BECAUSE IT BORE HIS OWN NAME AND ACCOUNT NUMBER*

"REX" A COLLIE OWNED BY ERNEST W. BUFFUM of Leeds, Me., HAS CAUGHT A ROLLED-UP NEWSPAPER TOSSED TO HIM FROM A MOVING TRAIN OF THE MAINE CENTRAL R.R. AND DELIVERED IT TO HIS MASTER *EVERY DAY FOR 11 YEARS*

THE DOOR OF THE OLD PRIORY OF MONKTON, in Pembroke, Wales, HAS HAD ITS LOCKS CHANGED MANY TIMES *- BUT ALWAYS FLIES OPEN IN THE DEAD OF NIGHT*

CAPT. SETH SILLIMAN of Black Rock, (now Bridgeport) Connecticut, WHO COMMANDED A BRITISH COMPANY IN 1741 IN THE INVASION OF CARTAGENA, COLOMBIA, RETIRED FROM THE ARMY AND RETURNED HOME *-AFTER SWAPPING HIS COMMISSION FOR A BARREL OF MOLASSES*

JOHN PRICE Vicar of Llanbedr-Painscastle, Wales, WAS SO FOND OF FRESH AIR THAT HIS VICARAGE FOR 6 YEARS CONSISTED *OF 3 PORTABLE BATH HOUSES* ONE SERVED AS HIS STUDY, A SECOND AS HIS BEDROOM AND THE THIRD AS HIS KITCHEN

THE **ARTIFICIAL LAKE**
in the Buen Retiro City Park,
in Madrid, Spain,

500 FEET LONG, **80** FEET WIDE,
AND **20** FEET DEEP, WAS CREATED
IN A PERIOD OF **10** DAYS TO
ENHANCE THE SETTING FOR THE
*WEDDING OF KING PHILIP II
TO HIS 4TH WIFE* (1568)

GIRLS
of the TANGUT TRIBE of Mongolia
*ARE FORBIDDEN TO WASH THEIR
FACES UNTIL THEY ARE MARRIED*

The **PULPIT**
in Brush Creek Church,
Pennsylvania,
*IS SHAPED LIKE
A WINE GLASS*

THE **OCTOPUS TREE**
Meru, Africa

THE CHURCH of ST. LEONARD
in Hazelwood, England,
IS THE ONLY CHURCH IN
GREAT BRITAIN IN WHICH
CATHOLIC SERVICES HAVE
BEEN HELD WITHOUT
INTERRUPTION FOR A
PERIOD OF 700 YEARS

*KING HENRY VIII LEFT THIS
ONE CHURCH UNDISTURBED
BECAUSE OF HIS HIGH
REGARD FOR THE VAVASOUR
FAMILY, WHICH WORSHIPED
THERE*

Bill PRATT (1810-1888)
of Williamstown, Mass.,
*ALWAYS WORE 7 SHIRTS AND
5 PAIRS OF TROUSERS*
IN SUMMER AS WELL AS
WINTER, AND KEPT A
BLAZING FIRE IN HIS ROOM

GRAPES on Lanzarote,
in the Canary Islands,
TO PROTECT THEM FROM
THE VIOLENT WINDS
*MUST BE GROWN IN HOLES IN
THE GROUND AND PROTECTED
FURTHER BY SEMICIRCULAR
STONE WALLS*

JOHANN PETER LYSER
(1803-1870) of Germany
WAS CELEBRATED AS A PAINTER, POET, MUSICIAN AND MUSIC CRITIC IN DRESDEN, VIENNA AND BERLIN FOR 33 YEARS
—YET THROUGHOUT THAT ENTIRE PERIOD HE WAS TOTALLY DEAF

THE ELM TREE GRAVE
Catherine de Bogart of Woodstock, N.Y., DIED AS A RESULT OF A BEATING AND WAS BURIED STILL GRASPING THE ELM TREE SWITCH
—WHICH GREW INTO A HUGE TREE THAT FORCED ITS WAY UP THROUGH HER GRAVESTONE

THE CAROLINUM
in Heidelberg, Germany, BUILT IN 1750 AS A SEMINARY AND NOW A COLLEGE DORMITORY
HAS BEEN USED AT VARIOUS TIMES AS A FACTORY, A HOSPITAL, AN ARMY BARRACKS, AN OFFICE BUILDING AND INSANE ASYLUM

PRINCESS TURIA and BEYOND
RACING AS A SINGLE ENTRY OF CALUMET FARM IN THE ACORN STAKES AT BELMONT PARK IN 1956
FINISHED IN A DEAD HEAT FOR FIRST PLACE

A TRIUMPHAL GATE
ERECTED FOR PRINCESS MARGARET'S VISIT TO MOMBASA, KENYA,
IN THE SHAPE OF 2 HUGE ELEPHANT TUSKS

AN ORPHAN
ADOPTED FROM A BUDAPEST ORPHANAGE IN 1920 BY ISTVAN TOROCSIK, A FARMER OF ALATTYAN, HUNGARY, WAS REVEALED YEARS LATER TO BE THE FARMER'S OWN GRANDDAUGHTER
– THE CHILD OF HIS DAUGHTER, ILONA, OF WHOM HE HAD LOST ALL TRACE

PIGGY BACK TREE
Madagascar
IT ALWAYS WRAPS ITSELF AROUND A NEIGHBORING TREE

VENUS' GIRDLE
A CREATURE OF THE SEA
IS 2 INCHES TALL AND 5 FEET WIDE AND 99 PER CENT WATER

The **LANTERN FLY**
of Dutch Guiana
IS NOT A FLY AND CASTS NO LIGHT—
IT IS A BUG, AND THE "LANTERN" PROTRUDING FROM ITS HEAD IS ALWAYS DARK

A **VIOLIN** USED BY THE **PAMPAS INDIANS** of Argentina *CONSISTING OF THE BOWED RIB OF A COLT AND A STRING MADE OF HORSEHAIR*

THE **GILRUTH HOUSE** in Yazoo City, Miss., WAS BUILT FOR HIS BRIDE BY SAMUEL WILSON IN CINCINNATI, OHIO, TAKEN APART AND TRANSPORTED BY STEAMBOAT 800 MILES — *AND THEN RE-ASSEMBLED ON ITS PRESENT LOCATION* — 1847 —

A **WIFE** in the Merina Tribe of Madagascar IS FORMALLY DIVORCED WHEN HER HUSBAND SAYS: *"I'LL GIVE YOU NO MORE MONEY!"*

A **HORSE RACE** WAS STAGED IN SEATTLE, WASH., ON JULY 22, 1881, BETWEEN TOM CLANCY AND ROBERT ABRAMS, WITH CITY AUTHORITIES CLEARING THE SITE FOR THEM *—BUT THE WINNER WAS ARRESTED AFTER THE RACE FOR EXCEEDING THE LEGAL SPEED LIMIT OF 6 MILES PER HOUR*

THE **POSTAGE CANCELLATION** in Chicago, Ill., IN 1870 *WAS A CASK MARKED "GIN"*

THE **GUILLEMOT** LAYS EGGS OF DIFFERENT COLORS —*NO TWO ALIKE*

GENERAL EMILIANO ZAPATA (1876-1919) MEXICAN REVOLUTIONIST— DESTROYED A QUARTER OF A BILLION DOLLARS WORTH OF PROPERTY *AND PERSONALLY KILLED 250 MEN!*

SENA A VILLAGE IN Hadhramaut, Arabia, *CONSISTS OF A SINGLE INHABITED ROCK*

"Secor" A PRIZE BULL OWNED BY THE LAZY L RANCH *HAS A PERMANENT SET OF FALSE TEETH* Florence, Texas

13 TOMBSTONES in Cooling, England, MARKING THE GRAVES OF THE COMPORT CHILDREN, ARE SHAPED LIKE LOZENGES— *THEIR FAVORITE CONFECTIONERY*

THE ANCIENT WALL

SURROUNDING THE RUINS OF ZIMBABWE, near Victoria, Africa, 30 FEET HIGH, 14 FEET WIDE, AND 800 FEET IN CIRCUMFERENCE, WAS BUILT WITHOUT MORTAR OF ANY KIND —

—YET IT HAS ENDURED FOR MORE THAN 500 YEARS

Captain Henry CLARK

1735 - 1836 of Bideford, England,

HEARTBROKEN BY THE DEATH OF HIS SWEETHEART **NEVER AGAIN ENTERED HIS HOUSE NOR SLEPT IN A BED FOR THE REMAINING 20 YEARS OF HIS LIFE**

The Statue

TO A CAT NAMED "Bouhaki" THE PET OF KING ANAA of Egypt 4,862 YEARS AGO —AND THE FIRST CAT IN HISTORY KNOWN TO HAVE A NAME

HIGH HORSEPOWER!

A COLLISION in San Juan, Puerto Rico, BETWEEN AN AUTOMOBILE AND A WAGON ENDED UP WITH THE HORSE ON TOP OF THE CAR'S ROOF
(JUNE 24, 1962)

49

GENERAL BARON von BENDER
1713 - 1798

WHO SERVED IN THE AUSTRIAN ARMY 64 YEARS

FOUGHT FOR HIS COUNTRY IN 29 WARS

GERARDINE and GUSTAVE SIMARD of Chicoutimi-Nord, Quebec, NAMED THEIR 15 CHILDREN:

G
IRARD
HISLAINE
ENEVIEVE
INETTE
HISLAIN
ABRIEL
EMMA
ERVAIS
LORIA
ERARDENE
UY
INA
UYLAINE
ERALD
UILLAUME

A **TEMPLE** to the **BRIDGE GOD** CONSTRUCTED ON A SPAN NEAR Chiang Chin, China, BY A BUILDER WHO BELIEVED IT WOULD *PROTECT ALL HIS FUTURE BRIDGES FROM COLLAPSING*

A **STATUE** OF A DOG in the Canary Islands REMINDS VISITORS THAT THE ISLANDS WERE SO NAMED *BECAUSE OF THEIR GREAT NUMBER OF DOGS* Canis is Latin for dog

FRIED FLYING ANTS
in the Kampala Market
in Africa
ARE SOLD AS A DELICACY

A **STUDENT** in China
TO QUALIFY AS A PHYSICIAN OR LAWYER *ONCE WAS REQUIRED TO PROVE HIS FITNESS BY BALANCING ON ONE FOOT WHILE USING THE OTHER FOOT* **TO PLACE A FEATHER ON HIS OWN HEAD**

THE **SUPREME COURT** of **TURKEY**
in Istanbul
LOCATED IN THE PALACE OF THE COUNCIL OF MINISTERS,
TO COMPLY WITH THE MOHAMMEDAN CONCEPTION OF JUSTICE **HAD NO DOORS FOR A PERIOD OF 357 YEARS**– ITS ENTRANCE WAS ALWAYS OPEN TO PETITIONERS

MRS. **FRED REEVES** of Midland, Mich.,
AT THE AGE OF 71 **SCORED A HOLE-IN-ONE IN HER FIRST GAME OF GOLF**

THE **EGG** OF THE PORT JACKSON SHARK HAS A SPIRAL SHELL *TO KEEP IT UPRIGHT IN THE RIVER BOTTOM AND PREVENT ITS BEING BURIED IN THE MUD*

A **TURNIP** IN THE SHAPE OF A SHRIVELED HAND IS REGARDED BY GERMAN FARMERS AS A SIGN THAT THEY WILL HAVE POOR CROPS

A **WOMAN** of the Nigerian Plateau, Africa, ADVERTISES THAT SHE IS WEALTHY BY WEARING A KEY AROUND HER NECK— USUALLY THE KEY WILL OPEN NO KNOWN LOCK -AND OFTEN THE WEARER HAS NEVER SEEN A LOCK

Edward CAPERN (1819-1895) BECAME FAMED AS A POET AS A RESULT OF POEMS HE COMPOSED WHILE MAKING HIS ROUNDS BETWEEN BIDEFORD AND BUCKLAND BREWER, England, *AS A LETTER CARRIER*

THE GLASS FISH (Ambasis lala) of India IS SO TRANSPARENT *IT LOOKS LIKE AN X-RAY*

52

MAGGIE LIBBY of North Bridgton, Me., HAVING LOST HER HAIR IN AN ILLNESS, *REFUSED TO LEAVE HER BED UNTIL IT GREW BACK* **20 YEARS LATER**

WAR MACES USED BY Kimbunda tribesmen of Africa **HAVE HEADS CARVED IN THE LIKENESS OF** *A QUEEN WHOM ALL MEN FEARED DURING HER LIFETIME*

BISSEL'S FERRY at Windsor, Conn., OPERATED CONTINUOUSLY FOR **260 YEARS**

GLOVES MANUFACTURED in Limerick, Ireland, 100 YEARS AGO WERE SO SHEER THAT A PAIR COULD BE STUFFED INTO A WALNUT SHELL

A **COW** OWNED BY ANDREW HOPKINS of Boyle, Ireland, GAVE BIRTH TO A "LITTER" OF **7 CALVES**

THE **TOWER** OF ST. MARY'S CHURCH, in East Bergholt, England, WAS LEFT UNCOMPLETED IN 1530 AND ITS BELLS ARE STILL HOUSED IN A TEMPORARY WOODEN STRUCTURE - 431 YEARS LATER

HENRY SHIVERNELL, of Columbia, S.C., HIT OVER THE HEART BY A RIFLE BULLET IN THE BATTLE OF CHURUBUSCO, IN THE MEXICAN WAR *WAS SAVED BY A BIBLE HE CARRIED IN HIS POCKET* (Aug. 20, 1847)

CAN'T SAY I DIDN'T TRY

HEN SAT ON A LIVE HAND GRENADE FOR **26** DAYS Marianas, 1945

GIRLS of Gafsa, Tunisia, TATTOO A CROSS ON EACH CHEEK *TO ANNOUNCE THEY ARE OLD ENOUGH TO MARRY*

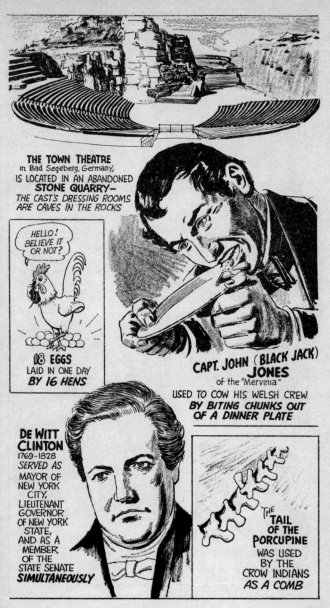

THE TOWN THEATRE in Bad Segeberg, Germany, IS LOCATED IN AN ABANDONED **STONE QUARRY —** *THE CAST'S DRESSING ROOMS ARE CAVES IN THE ROCKS*

HELLO! BELIEVE IT OR NOT?

18 EGGS LAID IN ONE DAY **BY 16 HENS**

CAPT. JOHN (BLACK JACK) JONES of the "Mervinia" USED TO COW HIS WELSH CREW *BY BITING CHUNKS OUT OF A DINNER PLATE*

DE WITT CLINTON 1769-1828 *SERVED AS* MAYOR OF NEW YORK CITY, LIEUTENANT GOVERNOR OF NEW YORK STATE, AND AS A MEMBER OF THE STATE SENATE **SIMULTANEOUSLY**

THE **TAIL** OF THE **PORCUPINE** WAS USED BY THE CROW INDIANS AS A COMB

THE MUSICAL ROCKS OF LES BAUX, France—THEY HAVE BEEN SO HOLLOWED OUT BY THE WEATHER THAT WINDS BLOWING THROUGH THEM PRODUCE MUSIC LIKE THAT *FROM AN AEOLIAN HARP*

THE JANISSARIES

MEMBERS OF A CRACK TURKISH ARMY CORPS WORE A SLEEVE AS THEIR HEADGEAR FOR 265 YEARS BECAUSE THEY WERE BLESSED IN 1561 BY A HOLY MAN *WHO PLACED ON THE HEAD OF ONE OF THEM HIS HAND IN A LONG SLEEVE*

ALEXANDER SETON
(1555 - 1622)
WAS NAMED PRIOR OF THE Pluscarden Monastery, Scotland, *AT THE AGE OF 10*

A DRUGSTORE in Strasbourg, France, HAS DONE BUSINESS CONTINUOUSLY AT THE SAME LOCATION *FOR 694 YEARS*

THE PEAK OF AMBITION
WOHENIE ROCK in Ethiopia,
6,500 FEET HIGH,
WAS USED UNTIL 100 YEARS
AGO AS A LOFTY EXILE FOR
ROYAL RELATIVES SUSPECTED
**OF PLOTTING FOR THE
EMPEROR'S THRONE**

GIRLS OF THE
XOSA TRIBE, in South Africa,
WEAR FRINGE OVER
THE FOREHEAD TO
**MAKE THEM
CROSS-EYED**

A
PARROT SAVED
THE LIFE
OF LEO, SON OF
EMPEROR BASIL
OF THE BYZANTINE
EMPIRE, WHO WAS
ABOUT TO BE
EXECUTED BY HIS
FATHER, BECAUSE THE
PARROT HAD BEEN
TRAINED TO CRY
"POOR LEO"
*EMPEROR BASIL SPARED
HIS SON AND LEO
BECAME RULER OF HALF
THE ROMAN WORLD
880*

THE **OLDEST TAVERN IN THE U.S.**
THE WHITE HOUSE TAVERN
in Newport, R.I.,
HAS BEEN OPERATING FOR 291 YEARS

A **RECLINING STATUE OF BUDDHA** IN POLONNARUWA, CEYLON, 80 FEET LONG *CARVED OUT OF SOLID ROCK*

The **NORTHERN SCALLOP** (Pecten Islandicus) IS CONSIDERED A FOOD DELICACY IN ICELAND, BUT IT IS DIFFICULT TO COOK BECAUSE *IT KEEPS JUMPING OUT OF THE POT*

THE GREAT WALL OF THE CHURCH OF TARTLAU, RUMANIA, CONSTRUCTED AS A PROTECTION AGAINST ATTACK, IS LINED WITH INDIVIDUAL CRIBS IN *WHICH EACH FARMER STORES HIS GRAIN*

THE HALFPENNY BRIDGE, Lechlade, England, *FOR CENTURIES ITS TOLL WAS JUST HALF A PENNY*

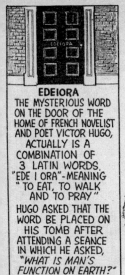

EDEIORA
THE MYSTERIOUS WORD ON THE DOOR OF THE HOME OF FRENCH NOVELIST AND POET VICTOR HUGO, ACTUALLY IS A COMBINATION OF 3 LATIN WORDS, "EDE I ORA"—MEANING "TO EAT, TO WALK AND TO PRAY"

HUGO ASKED THAT THE WORD BE PLACED ON HIS TOMB AFTER ATTENDING A SEANCE IN WHICH HE ASKED, *"WHAT IS MAN'S FUNCTION ON EARTH?"* AND THE ANSWER *"EDEIORA"* CAME TO HIM IN *"SPIRIT KNOCKS"*

THOMAS CROSS of Spelsbury, England, SEWED HIMSELF INTO HIS CLOTHING EACH MORNING AND UNDRESSED EACH NIGHT *BY RIPPING OPEN THE SEAMS*

SAMUEL FREEMAN MILLER
(1816-1890)
WAS A SUCCESSFUL PHYSICIAN UNTIL HE WAS 30 YEARS OF AGE, THEN DEVELOPED AN AVERSION TO MEDICINE AND TOOK UP LAW --BECOMING *AN ASSOCIATE JUSTICE OF THE U.S. SUPREME COURT*

THE **OLDEST KNOWN LATIN TEXT**
A MEMORIAL STONE FOUND IN ROME, ITALY, BEARING A WARNING NOT TO DESECRATE THE AREA -- *WAS ENGRAVED IN LATIN 2,650 YEARS AGO*

Bob Hewitt of Hannington, England, DRANK A FULL GALLON OF ALE IN THE LOCAL INN EVERY NIGHT

WHILE SUSPENDED FROM A HOOK IN THE TAVERN'S CEILING

A COCKROACH IS CALLED A "RUSSIAN" IN PRUSSIA AND A "PRUSSIAN" IN RUSSIA

AN ACRE OF LAND WHICH A BEGGAR NAMED 'DOG' SMITH BEQUEATHED TO The Church of Lambeth, England, WITH THE STIPULATION THAT IT CARE FOR HIS DOG AFTER SMITH'S DEATH *TODAY BRINGS THE CHURCH A RENTAL OF $405,000 A YEAR—* IT IS THE SITE OF THE LONDON COUNTY HALL, HEADQUARTERS OF THE LONDON COUNTY COUNCIL.

THE GOVERNMENT HOUSE in Andorra SERVES SIMULTANEOUSLY AS *A MUSEUM, A PRISON, A CHURCH, PARLIAMENT AND AN INN*

WALNUTS FROM TREES MORE THAN 100 YEARS OLD OFTEN HAVE SHELLS DIVIDED INTO 3 OR EVEN 4 PARTS

HORSES WERE SOLD in Australia in 1924 **FOR ONE CENT EACH**

John Edward WILKINSON of Wilmurt, N.Y., WHOSE ENGAGEMENT WAS BROKEN IN 1829 ON THE DAY HE WAS TO HAVE BEEN MARRIED, WAS BURIED IN HIS WEDDING SUIT *WHICH HE HAD STORED IN MOTHBALLS FOR 50 YEARS*

THE **MEMORIAL TO FALSE PRIDE** **BROTHER MATTEO** WHO BUILT THE PORCH OF GLORY LEADING TO THE SANCTUARY OF Santiago de Compostela, Spain, TO ATONE FOR HIS PRIDE OVER THE HIGH PRAISE FOR HIS WORK *ADDED A STATUE OF HIMSELF ON HIS KNEES BEATING HIS BREAST IN REPENTANCE*

WHITE BIRCH GROWING OUT OF A *HONEY LOCUST TREE*

61

2 CROWS HAVE APPEARED on Temple Hill, near Madras, India, TO BE FED BY A WAITING HOLY MAN AT THE SAME HOUR EACH DAY FOR MORE *THAN 1,200 YEARS*

POTTERY REPRODUCTIONS OF THE ROYAL OAK OF BOSCOBEL, England, IN WHICH KING CHARLES II HID FROM CROMWELL'S SOLDIERS, WERE FORBIDDEN TO ENGLISH SUBJECTS FOR YEARS *UNDER PAIN OF DEATH*

LUCY HUTCHINSON (1620-1673) THE PURITAN WRITER COULD REPEAT FROM MEMORY FOR HER FATHER'S SERVANTS ANY SERMON SHE HAD HEARD - *WHEN SHE WAS ONLY 4 YEARS OF AGE*

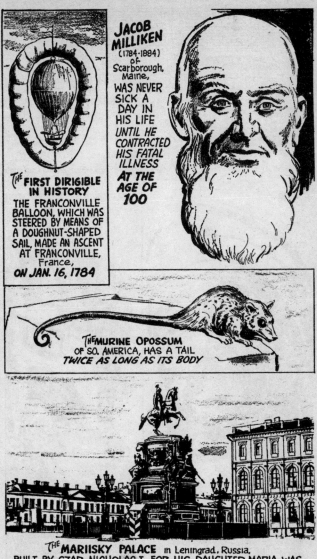

JACOB MILLIKEN (1784-1884) of Scarborough, Maine, WAS NEVER SICK A DAY IN HIS LIFE *UNTIL HE CONTRACTED HIS FATAL ILLNESS* AT THE AGE OF **100**

THE **FIRST DIRIGIBLE IN HISTORY** THE FRANCONVILLE BALLOON, WHICH WAS STEERED BY MEANS OF A DOUGHNUT-SHAPED SAIL, MADE AN ASCENT AT FRANCONVILLE, France, **ON JAN. 16, 1784**

THE **MURINE OPOSSUM** OF SO. AMERICA, HAS A TAIL *TWICE AS LONG AS ITS BODY*

THE **MARIISKY PALACE** in Leningrad. Russia, BUILT BY CZAR NICHOLAS I FOR HIS DAUGHTER, MARIA, WAS ABANDONED BY MARIA IN 1859 BECAUSE A STATUE OF HER FATHER *HAD ITS BACK TURNED TOWARD THE PALACE*

THE **TOWN** OF **WIDOWS**
Cervo, Italy
EVERY MAN IN THE VILLAGE
--150 FISHERMEN--
PERISHED IN ONE STORM!

AHMAD PASHA al-**JAZZAR**
Turkish governor of Syria and Lebanon
IRKED BY A DISAGREEMENT
WITH ONE OF HIS WIVES
*HAD ALL 37 OF HIS WIVES
BURNED ALIVE!*

THE **LITTLE CHURCH** of
the **WILDERNESS**
in the Canton of Appenzell,
Switzerland,
WAS CONSTRUCTED IN 1656
*DEEP INSIDE A
STALACTITE CAVE*

A **LIGHT** BURNS AT THE STONE COUCH IN THE PALACE OF ERANIEL, INDIA, TO GUIDE BACK A MAHARAJAH OF TRAVANCORE WHO VANISHED MYSTERIOUSLY WHILE SLEEPING ON THE COUCH **433 YEARS AGO**

X. NOEL of Nimes, France, BECAME THE FATHER OF QUADRUPLETS ON **Christmas Day**

HE NAMED THEM:
HEUREUX -- HAPPY
FORTUNE -- FORTUNATE
FELIX --- FELICITOUS
GAI ---- GAY

We wish a happy, fortunate, felicitous and gay Christmas to all our readers everywhere!

GRACE CHURCH in Hirschberg, Silesia, WAS BUILT IN 1709 AT A COST OF $250,000 -OF WHICH $200,000 WAS A BRIBE TO EMPEROR JOSEPH I TO PERMIT ITS CONSTRUCTION

THE BEACH OF MAIO in the Windward Islands IS SURROUNDED BY SALT WATER —YET DIGGING DOWN ONLY **6 FEET PRODUCES A WELL OF SWEET WATER**

A **STRAW HAT** in Zinacantlan, Mexico, **IS USED TO MEASURE DISTANCES** NATIVES WEAVE THE HATS WHILE WALKING FROM PLACE TO PLACE —AND **INDICATE DISTANCES BY THE NUMBER OF HATS THEY CAN COMPLETE**

A **FIDDLE** USED BY FRENCH DANCING TEACHERS in the 18th century **WAS FITTED WITH A FAN**

THE GREAT ICE CAVE OF CHAUX-les-PASSAVANT. in France, IS FILLED WITH ICE THROUGHOUT THE YEAR —BUT ALWAYS CONTAINS MORE ICE AFTER A MILD WINTER

THE TRIBE of JOHNNY-ONE-NOTES
MUSICIANS AMONG THE Chamula Indians of Mexico *PLAY THE SAME MELODY AT FIESTAS, WEDDINGS AND FUNERALS*

The **TOMBSTONE** of ROBERT L. MUSGROVE near Winfield, Illinois, WHO WAS KILLED SHORTLY BEFORE HE WAS TO HAVE BEEN WED, HAS BEEN MARKED BY NATURE WITH THE OUTLINE *OF A YOUNG LADY KNEELING IN PRAYER*

Will you marry me?

A MARRIAGE PROPOSAL WRITTEN BY THOMAS EMMOT, OF LANCASHIRE, ENGLAND, *ON A MATCHBOX, DURING A BUS RIDE, AS HIS PROPOSAL OF MARRIAGE—* HIS SWEETHEART WROTE, "YES" ON THE SAME MATCHBOX—*AND THEY LIVED HAPPILY EVER AFTER*

THE ICE LARKSPUR (Delphinium Glaciale) *IS THE HIGHEST GROWING PLANT—* IT HAS BEEN FOUND ON Mt. Kanchanjanga, in the Himalayas, AT AN ALTITUDE OF 25,000 FEET

THE HARSHEST TAX IN ALL HISTORY

RANJIT SINGH CONQUEROR OF PESHAWAR in Northern India, FOR A PERIOD OF 21 YEARS EXACTED AS A TAX *THE SEVERED HEADS OF 100 MEN A YEAR*

A CABIN
BUILT FOR WEARY TRAVELERS on Mount Cacallo, Corsica, *INSIDE A HUGE BOULDER*

A BOUQUET OF VIOLETS
PICKED BY DEBRA PEARCY OUTSIDE HER HOME in Indianapolis, Ind., *IN OCTOBER*

THE INDIAN MANTIS
LOOKS SO MUCH LIKE A BRILLIANTLY HUED FLOWER THAT SMALLER INSECTS LAND ON IT — AND ARE PROMPTLY DEVOURED

PRAYER BOOKS
in medieval Germany WERE BOUND IN LEATHER POUCHES *SO THEY COULD BE FASTENED TO A MAN'S BELT FOR CONVENIENT REFERENCE*

AN ICEBERG

OBSERVED IN THE ARCTIC OCEAN BY THE PARRY EXPEDITION *WAS SHAPED LIKE A GOTHIC TEMPLE* 1824

MALMAISON in Greenwood, Miss., WAS BUILT FOR COL. GREENWOOD LEFLORE, A CHOCTAW INDIAN CHIEF, BY JAMES CLARK HARRIS, WHO DEMANDED AND RECEIVED AS HIS FEE *THE HAND OF COL. LEFLORE'S DAUGHTER* (1854)

The **STRANGEST COIFFURES ARE WORN BY MEN!**

MASHUKULUMBWE TRIBESMEN of Africa WEAR THEIR HAIR, REINFORCED BY THE ADDITION OF THE HAIR OF ALL FEMALE RELATIVES, IN A HEADDRESS SO HIGH THAT *THEY MUST SLEEP WITH THE COIFFURE TIED TO THE CEILING*

COSPAIA
A VILLAGE in Italy
HAD ONLY 100 INHABITANTS
-YET IT WAS AN INDEPENDENT REPUBLIC FOR 41 YEARS
(1785-1826)

CHESIL BEACH near Portland, Eng.
18 MILES LONG
DOES NOT HAVE 2 PEBBLES ALIKE
CITY OFFICIALS OF PORTLAND ONCE OFFERED A REWARD TO ANYONE WHO COULD FIND 2 MATCHING PEBBLES

WOMEN REFUGEES
FLEEING TO Pakistan from Kazakhstan, Russia, CONVERT THEIR ENTIRE FORTUNES INTO GOLD AND SILVER MEDALLIONS WHICH ARE SEWN ON THEIR DRESSES

THE **OTTONEUM** in Kassel, Germany, WAS THE FIRST THEATRE BUILDING ERECTED IN ALL GERMANY
IT WAS BUILT IN 1604 FOR A TRAVELING GROUP OF ENGLISH SHAKESPEAREAN ACTORS, AND HAS BEEN USED AS A CHURCH, A FOUNDRY, A TAX OFFICE, A COLLEGE AND MUSEUM.

MAILBOATS in Hangchow, China, ARE STILL ROWED BY *BOTH HANDS AND FEET*

LIVIA (12 B.C.- 31 A.D.)
DAUGHTER-IN-LAW OF EMPEROR TIBERIUS OF ROME, POISONED HER HUSBAND, DRUSUS *AND WAS IN TURN STARVED TO DEATH BY HER OWN MOTHER*

THE **FIRST "BUCK"**
A DOLLAR, ISSUED BY Wallowa County, Oregon, in 1933 *WAS PRINTED ON BUCKSKIN*

THE **PERSIAN MONARCH** near Meiruba, Lebanon, *CARVED BY NATURE*

THE WORLD'S FIRST CITY TO BE LIT ENTIRELY BY ELECTRICITY WAS AURORA, ILLINOIS 1882

CANARIES ORIGINALLY WERE **BROWN** YELLOW CANARIES ARE DESCENDANTS OF 2 FREAK BIRDS

THE MONARCH WHO COULD NOT ESCAPE HIS FATE!

KING FERDINAND V (1452-1516) HUSBAND OF THE SPANISH QUEEN WHO FINANCED COLUMBUS, NEVER VISITED MADRIGAL, HIS WIFE'S BIRTHPLACE, BECAUSE *A SOOTHSAYER TOLD HIM HE WOULD DIE IN MADRIGAL*

HE FELL ILL IN A LITTLE VILLAGE, LEARNED THAT ITS NAME WAS LITTLE MADRIGAL --*AND DIED OF FRIGHT*

THE **ELGIN CATHEDRAL** IN MORAY, SCOTLAND, CONSTRUCTED IN 1224, WAS RUINED IN 1568 WHEN ITS *LEAD ROOF WAS STRIPPED OFF TO PAY THE SCOTTISH ARMY*

THE REV. ANTOINE GONNET (1765-1847) CURATE OF ARFEUILLES, FRANCE, BEING TRUNDLED TO THE GUILLOTINE BY REVOLUTIONARIES IN 1794 WAS RESCUED BY A GROUP OF HIS PARISHIONERS *DISGUISED AS WOMEN*

HORSE LOVERS IN 17th CENTURY SWITZERLAND DRANK WINE FROM GOBLETS SHAPED *LIKE A KNIGHT ON A REARING CHARGER*

A CEDAR TREE GROWING FROM THE CROTCH OF A MAPLE TREE

ROOT IN THE SHAPE OF A *PITCHER* FOUND ON THE SCHOENBORN FARM, NEAR OREGON CITY, OREGON

ROBERT MORRIS (1734-1806) A SIGNER OF THE DECLARATION OF INDEPENDENCE *HAD VOTED AGAINST THE DECLARATION IN CONGRESS!*

73

THE BARLEY MOW AN INN in CLIFTON HAMPDEN, ENGLAND, *WAS BUILT AROUND PAIRS OF BOWED TREES WHICH SUPPORTED THE RIDGE POLE AND ROOF* THE STRUCTURE HAS BEEN STANDING FOR MORE THAN **600** YEARS

THE DUKE de POLIGNAC (1780-1847) FRENCH PRIME MINISTER UNDER KING CHARLES X, SAVED FROM ARREST BY A LAUNDRYMAN NAMED ANCELIN, SHOWED HIS GRATITUDE BY CHANGING HIS NAME TO ANCELIN-POLIGNAC *--EVEN THOUGH HE WAS EVENTUALLY CAPTURED AND IMPRISONED*

A **HUGE TOM-TOM** LONG USED BY THE NGONI TRIBE OF AFRICA AS A CALL TO PAGAN RITES IS NOW BEATEN TO CALL THE TRIBESMEN **TO CHURCH SERVICES**

THE GATE
OF THE CASTLE OF TÜBINGEN, GERMANY,
IS AN ORNATE MEMORIAL TO THE
HONOR BESTOWED BY A KING
OF ENGLAND IN 1603 ON
DUKE FREDERICK OF WÜRTTEMBERG
--*THE ORDER OF THE GARTER*

2 TREES
GROWING
OUT OF A
*ROOF-TOP
GUTTER*

A NATIVE OF CANTON
DURING CHINA'S DISASTROUS FLOOD
OF 1931, NEGOTIATED STREETS THAT
WERE UNDER 30 FEET OF WATER
*USING AS A BOAT HIS COFFIN
-- CONSTRUCTED IN PREPARATION
FOR HIS OWN FUNERAL*

THE TOWN HALL of Neidenburg, Poland,
DAMAGED BY BOMBS IN WORLD WAR II WHEN IT WAS PART OF GERMANY,
FUNCTIONED AS THE CITY'S SEAT OF GOVERNMENT FOR 20 YEARS
WITHOUT DOORS OR WINDOWS

THE MOSQUE OF SULTAN SOLIMAN in Istanbul, Turkey, WAS BUILT IN 1549 WITH 4 MINARETS - BECAUSE HE WAS THE 4TH RULER FOLLOWING THE CONQUEST OF ISTANBUL - AND WITH 10 GALLERIES - BECAUSE HE WAS THE 10TH RULER IN HIS FAMILY

THE REV. AMARIAH CHANDLER (1782-1864) of Wartsfield, Vermont, A MINISTER FOR 54 YEARS ALWAYS WALKED TO CHURCH BAREFOOTED DONNING HIS BOOTS ONLY WHEN HE REACHED THE EDIFICE

THE AMERICAN LEGATION in Baghdad, Iraq, IS A MINIATURE REPLICA OF THE WHITE HOUSE IN WASHINGTON, D.C.

HIRAM F. SMITH
A LEGISLATOR IN THE STATE
OF WASHINGTON, ALSO WORKED AS
*A PRINTER, PUBLISHER, BUTCHER,
EXPRESSMAN, MAIL CARRIER,
ORCHARDIST AND RANCHER*

THE **CHURCH OF ST. NICHOLAS**
in Bari, Italy,
WHICH HOLDS THE BODY OF
SANTA CLAUS, WAS UNDER
CONSTRUCTION FOR 110 YEARS,
BECAUSE THE ITALIAN SAILORS
WHO KIDNAPED THE REMAINS
FROM A TOMB IN MYRA, ASIA,
INSISTED SANTA CLAUS NEEDED
*TIME TO BECOME ACCLIMATED
TO HIS NEW HOME*

THE MOST ELABORATE DEATH TRAP IN HISTORY Baghdad, Iraq,
A PALACE, BUILT IN 754 FOR ABDALLAH ben ALI, THE GOVERNOR OF SYRIA,
BY HIS NEPHEW, CALIPH MANSUR, WAS **CONSTRUCTED ON A FOUNDATION OF SALT**
*A STREAM OF WATER WAS THEN DIVERTED TO UNDERMINE
THE STRUCTURE--WHICH BURIED ITS OCCUPANTS IN THE RUINS*

THE WATER LILY
KEEPS ITS BUDS UNDERWATER UNTIL THEY ARE READY TO BLOOM WHEN THE FLOWERS FADE AND POLLINATION IS COMPLETED THE STEM DIPS UNDERWATER TO ENABLE THE SEEDPODS TO RIPEN BENEATH THE SURFACE

BISMARCK
AS A STUDENT AT THE UNIVERSITY OF GÖTTINGEN *FOUGHT 28 DUELS*

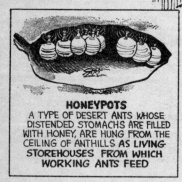

HONEYPOTS
A TYPE OF DESERT ANTS WHOSE DISTENDED STOMACHS ARE FILLED WITH HONEY, ARE HUNG FROM THE CEILING OF ANTHILLS **AS LIVING STOREHOUSES** FROM WHICH WORKING ANTS FEED

DR. GERRIT PARMELE JUDD
(1803-1873) A PHYSICIAN AND MISSIONARY SUCCESSIVELY SERVED KING KAMEHAMEHA III OF HAWAII AS *MINISTER OF FOREIGN AFFAIRS, MINISTER OF THE INTERIOR, AND MINISTER OF FINANCE*

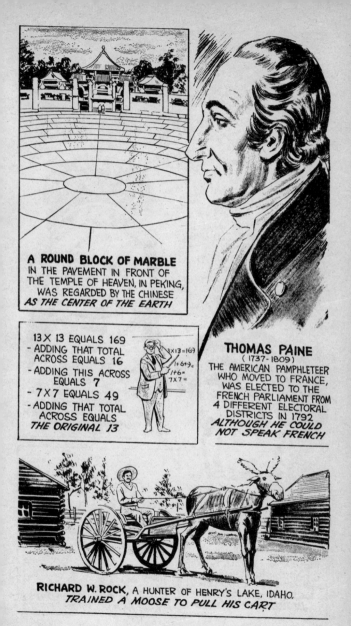

A ROUND BLOCK OF MARBLE
IN THE PAVEMENT IN FRONT OF
THE TEMPLE OF HEAVEN, IN PEKING,
WAS REGARDED BY THE CHINESE
AS THE CENTER OF THE EARTH

13 X 13 EQUALS 169
- ADDING THAT TOTAL
ACROSS EQUALS 16
- ADDING THIS ACROSS
EQUALS 7
- 7 X 7 EQUALS 49
- ADDING THAT TOTAL
ACROSS EQUALS
THE ORIGINAL 13

THOMAS PAINE
(1737 - 1809)
THE AMERICAN PAMPHLETEER
WHO MOVED TO FRANCE,
WAS ELECTED TO THE
FRENCH PARLIAMENT FROM
4 DIFFERENT ELECTORAL
DISTRICTS IN 1792
*ALTHOUGH HE COULD
NOT SPEAK FRENCH*

RICHARD W. ROCK, A HUNTER OF HENRY'S LAKE, IDAHO,
TRAINED A MOOSE TO PULL HIS CART

THE CASTLE THAT WAS A PROPHECY OF DEATH!

KING RICHARD III AS A BOY WAS WARNED BY A SOOTHSAYER THAT HE WOULD DIE **SOON AFTER HE GAZED UPON ROUGEMONT**

THE MONARCH WAS STARTLED ONE DAY TO LEARN THAT A CASTLE HE WAS ADMIRING WAS NAMED ROUGEMONT — AND SUBSEQUENTLY, IN AUGUST, 1485 HE WAS SLAIN IN BATTLE!

Exeter, England

WOMEN

of the Humbe Region of Angola, Portuguese Africa, ALWAYS FIX THEIR HAIR IN A COIFFURE *COPIED FROM AN EARLY AIRMAN'S HELMET*

THOMAS HOWARD

(1536-1572) WHO BECAME THE DUKE OF NORFOLK IN 1554, FOR THE 18 YEARS UNTIL HE WAS BEHEADED *WAS THE ONLY DUKE IN ALL ENGLAND*

THE MONKEY DRUM

of Xicotepec, Mexico, A RELIC OF THE ANCIENT AZTEC PAGANS, *IS STILL PLAYED ONCE A YEAR AT A NOCTURNAL FIESTA*

FLORAL DESIGNS WHICH WERE DISPLAYED IN FRAMES, WERE MADE IN THE 19th CENTURY *FROM HUMAN HAIRS*

THE **POOR BOX** OUTSIDE THE ADMIRALTY CHURCH OF KARLSKRONA, SWEDEN, IS A SCULPTURE OF AN OLD MAN, AND BEARS THE INSCRIPTION: *"LIFT UP MY HAT AND GIVE ME A COIN"*

THE VICTORIA GATE IN DUNDEE, SCOTLAND, WAS ERECTED IN 1844 TO SERVE ONLY ONE DAY AS AN ARCH FOR QUEEN VICTORIA'S VISIT *--BUT HAS REMAINED AS A MEMORIAL FOR 128 YEARS*

THE **PARASITIC HOPLISUS WASP** INVADES THE NEST OF THE REGULAR HOPLISUS WASP-- LAYS ITS EGGS WHERE ITS HATCHED YOUNG WILL KILL THE OFFSPRING OF ITS HOST *--AND SLIPS BACK OUT OF THE NEST WITHOUT LEAVING A SIGN OF ITS INTRUSION*

WILLIAM SHORT (1759-1849) ADOPTED SON OF THOMAS JEFFERSON WAS THE FIRST OFFICIAL APPOINTED UNDER THE U.S. CONSTITUTION *HE WAS COMMISSIONED BY PRESIDENT WASHINGTON IN 1789 TO SERVE AS MINISTER TO FRANCE*

BURNHAM
-BY-THE-SEA
A 50-ROOM STRUCTURE
in Washington, D.C.,
WAS DISMANTLED AND
TRANSPORTED TO NEWPORT, R.I.
-WHERE IT NOW SERVES
AS A GIRLS' SCHOOL

THE BALANCING BOULDER
near Buhl, Idaho
A ROCK 40 FEET HIGH
PERCHED ON A SMALL STONE

Governor LICINUS
of ancient Gaul
DIVIDED THE YEAR
INTO 14 MONTHS
-TO ASSURE HIM 2
EXTRA TAX COLLECTIONS

THE HORNED SCREAMER
of Brazil
HAS A HORN
ON ITS HEAD
AND SPURS ON
ITS WINGS

THE **BENNETT-BOARDMAN** HOUSE in Saugus, Mass., HAS NEVER BEEN MOVED— YET IT HAS BEEN LOCATED IN 2 COUNTIES AND 4 TOWNS

THE **2D EARL of MANCHESTER** 1602-1671 WAS SO FOND OF THE EARL OF WARWICK THAT HE SUCCESSIVELY MARRIED THE EARL OF WARWICK'S NIECE, HIS SISTER — *AND FINALLY HIS WIDOW*

THE **TOWERS** of the Cathedral of Jakarta, in Indonesia, ARE MADE OF SOLID IRON

A **cat** OWNED BY MRS. R.A. STUBENVOLL *JUMPS INTO AN OPEN GLASS JAR WHENEVER ITS OWNER FEEDS THE TROPICAL FISH* Dallas, Texas

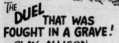

THE **DUEL** THAT WAS FOUGHT IN A GRAVE!

CLAY ALLISON, FAMED PIONEER of New Mexico, AND JAMES JOHNSON, A NEIGHBOR, SETTLED A QUARREL OVER WATER RIGHTS BY DIGGING A DEEP GRAVE AND THEN FIGHTING A DUEL TO THE DEATH IN IT – *WITH BOWIE KNIVES!*

JOHNSON NEVER LEFT THE GRAVE AND ALLISON SUFFERED WOUNDS WHICH CAUSED HIM TO LIMP ALL THE REST OF HIS LIFE

Prince **AUGUSTUS**
(1696-1763) of Saxony BECAME PRESIDENT OF THE UNIVERSITY OF WITTENBERG, Germany, *WHEN HE WAS ONLY 5 YEARS OF AGE!*

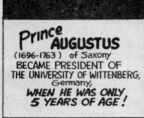

FISHING VESSELS of Romagna, Italy, SINCE THE DAYS OF THE ANCIENT ROMAN EMPIRE *HAVE EYES PAINTED AROUND THEIR HAWSER HOLES TO HELP THEM FIND THEIR WAY*

WOMEN of Ladakh, India, COMB THEIR HAIR *ONLY ONCE EACH YEAR—* THEIR ELABORATE COIFFURES ARE CREATED AFTER THE ANNUAL HARVEST AND ARE NOT TOUCHED AGAIN FOR 12 MONTHS

A SHEPHERD'S HUT near Claparedes, France, BUILT WITHOUT MORTAR *—YET IT HAS REMAINED INTACT FOR 1,000 YEARS*

HATCHET FISH WHICH LIVE IN THE DEEPEST PART OF THE OCEAN, *HAVE EYES WHICH CAN ONLY LOOK UPWARD*

ANTHILL NEAR MUKDISHU, SOMALILAND, IN THE SHAPE OF A DUCK

THE RIVER TERN HATCHES ITS EGGS *WHILE ITS REED NEST FLOATS WITH THE CURRENT*

THE **WINDMILL** of **REIGATE**, England, *HAS BEEN CONVERTED INTO A CHURCH IN WHICH SERVICES ARE HELD REGULARLY*

THE **MOST SENSITIVE MAN IN ALL HISTORY!** **CHARLES FANE** BRITISH ENVOY TO FLORENCE, ITALY, *BECAME DESPERATELY ILL FOR 6 WEEKS* BECAUSE THE BRITISH FOREIGN SECRETARY IN A LETTER TO FANE, OMITTED THE WORD "VERY" IN SIGNING IT – *"Your (very) humble servant"*

A MONUMENT ON A ROAD IN PERU BETWEEN LIMA AND CALLAO IS TOPPED BY A WRECKED AUTO AND BEARS THE INSCRIPTION:
"THE SLOWER YOU TRAVEL THE FURTHER YOU'LL JOURNEY"

DESPACIO SE VA LEJOS
ROTARY CLUB

DENIS O'HAMPSAY (1695-1807)
A BLIND HARPIST of Magilligan, Ireland,
WHO WAS UNABLE TO OPEN HIS EYES FOR 109 YEARS SUDDENLY FOUND HE COULD OPEN THEM WIDE WHILE PLAYING THE HARP AT THE AGE OF 112
– BUT A MOMENT LATER DIED WITH HIS HANDS ON THE HARP

THE GREAT CASTLE of HIROSAKI in Japan HAS STOOD FOR MORE THAN 300 YEARS
– YET ITS FOUNDATION CONSISTS ONLY OF A PILE OF LOOSE STONES WITHOUT MORTAR

MRS. RAY C. SCHOENHERR of Detroit, Mich., IS THE MOTHER OF 7 CHILDREN

JEANNETTE, BORN ON A MONDAY
KATHLEEN, BORN ON A TUESDAY
SUZANNE, BORN ON A WEDNESDAY
ANDREW, BORN ON A THURSDAY
THOMAS, BORN ON A FRIDAY
MARY, BORN ON A SATURDAY
JOSEPH, BORN ON A SUNDAY

MRS. MICHAELINE JALKOSKY
of Philadelphia, Pa.,
WAS BORN ON *SEPTEMBER 29,* 1919,
HER DAUGHTER, BARBARA, WAS
BORN *SEPTEMBER 29,* 1939,
HER GRANDDAUGHTER, THERESA,
WAS BORN *SEPTEMBER 29,* 1965

THE FRIGATE BIRD
WHICH HAS A WINGSPAN
OF 7 FEET
*HAS A SKELETON THAT WEIGHS
LESS THAN ITS FEATHERS*

THE
LEAF BUG
of So. America
AS A DISGUISE
AGAINST ITS
ENEMIES HAS
*HIND LEGS WITH
"CALVES" SHAPED LIKE LEAVES*

KING CHARLES II
(1248-1309) of Naples
WAS THE FATHER OF
SAINT LOUIS BERTRAND,
KING CHARLES OF HUNGARY,
KING ROBERT OF SICILY,
EMPEROR PHILIPPE
OF CONSTANTINOPLE,
QUEEN ELEANOR OF SICILY,
QUEEN MARGUERITE OF
PROVENCE AND QUEEN
BLANCHE OF ARAGON

A
WINDOW 12 INCHES HIGH AND 10
INCHES WIDE, IN THE TEMPLE
IN MASSYAF, SYRIA, WHICH
CONTAINS THE TOMB OF
REVERED SHEIK YUSSEF RABHO
SERVES AS THE LOCAL LIE
DETECTOR - *THE CULPRIT OR
LITIGANT WHO IS TELLING AN
UNTRUTH FINDS HIMSELF
UNABLE TO CRAWL THROUGH
THE WINDOW-REGARDLESS OF
THE SMALLNESS OF HIS FRAME*

PASSENGERS DISEMBARKING FROM BOATS IN THE HARBOR of Mogadishu, Somaliland, ARE SWUNG TO THE ROCKY SHORE *IN A HUGE CANVAS BAG*

ELEPHANTS HAVE RIGHT OF WAY

ROAD SIGN in Queen Elizabeth National Park, Uganda

THE **BASIN** OF THE FOUNTAIN of Santa Sabina, in Rome, Italy, *WAS ORIGINALLY USED AS A BATHTUB 1,600 YEARS AGO.*

THE STONE GOD

A **CLIFF** on the Irrawaddy River, Burma, IS CLIMBED EACH YEAR BY WORSHIPERS BECAUSE THE FIGURE ON THE STEEP ROCK IS CONSIDERED *A NATURAL CARVING OF A GOD*

THE OLDEST PIECE OF WOODEN FURNITURE

A CUPBOARD IN THE monastery of Obazine, France, *WAS CONSTRUCTED 800 YEARS AGO*

THE 5th **LORD HEADLEY** (1855-1935) AN ENGLISH PEER WHO BECAME A MOHAMMEDAN - 3 TIMES REFUSED TO BE CROWNED KING OF ALBANIA -*BECAUSE HE PREFERRED TO DIE IN HIS ENGLISH BED*

THE **DUKE** OF **CAXIAS** (1803-1880) FAMED SOLDIER AND STATESMAN *WAS THE ONLY BRAZILIAN DUKE IN THE COUNTRY'S HISTORY*

RICHARD BUSBY
(1606-1695) was at Westminster School, in London, England, AS A PUPIL AND MASTER *FOR 69 YEARS*

THE **TRAVEMUNDE LIGHTHOUSE** Germany
IS 115 FEET HIGH - YET IT WAS BUILT BY DUTCH MASONS IN 1539 WITHOUT THE USE OF SCAFFOLDING

V.Y. RICHARDSON of Dallas, Texas, AT THE AGE OF 65 CAN ROLL 6 HUGE TRUCK TIRES A DISTANCE OF 75 FEET *WITH ONE HAND*

THE ROYAL CHAPEL in Palermo, Italy, IS SO CONSTRUCTED THAT THE SUN'S RAYS SHINE THROUGH ITS DOME FOR ONLY ONE HOUR EACH DAY -*FROM NOON TO 1 P.M.*

MAULAWI MOHAMMED
Prime Minister of Bhopal, India, from 1860 to 1883, FOR THE ENTIRE PERIOD OF 23 YEARS MADE A WEEKLY ROUND TRIP BETWEEN BHOPAL AND INDORE- *COMPLETING THE 200 MILES IN 16 HOURS -ON A CAMEL*

THE INDIAN ALMOND TREE GROWS ITS BRANCHES ON A PERFECT HORIZONTAL PLANE --*AND THEY ALWAYS POINT NORTH AND SOUTH*

THE "COMPASS" TREE

* from an old print

THE WITCHES' MUSHROOMS
(Hebeloma crustuliniforme) ALWAYS *GROW IN A "MAGIC CIRCLE"*

92

THE TOWN THAT HAS 7 NEW YEARS

KALIMPONG, A COMMUNITY in India with 79,000 RESIDENTS, CELEBRATES A DIFFERENT NEW YEAR'S DAY —WITH EQUAL VERVE—FOR ITS *EUROPEAN, LOSSAR, CHINESE, MERWARI, NEPALESE, MOSLEM AND LEPCHA TOWNSMEN*

GIOVANNI PAPIS
AN INNKEEPER OF Mendrisio, Switzerland, NEVER REMOVED HIS BROWN DERBY DURING HIS ADULT LIFETIME —AND *WAS BURIED WITH IT ON*

JAMES RENWICK Jr. (1818-1895)
Designer of St. Patrick's Cathedral in New York City

NEVER STUDIED ARCHITECTURE AND NEVER SAW A GOTHIC STRUCTURE UNTIL HE HAD **DESIGNED ONE HIMSELF !**

NANCY WILLIE

"A POSTMAN of Askrigg, England,

WAS SO TERRIFIED OF WOMEN THAT HE WOULD NEVER DELIVER MAIL TO THEM –

AFTER HIS DEATH HIS ROOM WAS FOUND STACKED WITH SUCH UNDELIVERED LETTERS –

POSTMARKED OVER A PERIOD OF 21 YEARS

HELLO– BELIEVE IT OR NOT!

A SIAMESE CAT OWNED BY GEORGE BISHOP HAD ONE LITTER OF 4 KITTENS – EACH WITH 6 TOES ON EACH FRONT PAW – AND A SECOND LITTER OF 4 KITTENS – EACH WITH 5 TOES ON EACH FRONT PAW
Palo Alto, Calif.

THE SPIRE of the Church of St. Sulpice, in Fougères, France,
HAS LEANED 18 INCHES OFF CENTER FOR 322 YEARS

A SORCERER NAMED POUSSINIERE, SENTENCED TO DEATH, PREDICTED THE SPIRE WOULD SO SLANT – AND IT TILTED ON THE DAY HE WAS BURNED AT THE STAKE

"Wer seinen Kindern giebt das Brot und leidet nachmals selber Noth, den schlage man mit der Keule todt."

"If a man gives his bread to his children and then suffers want, take this club and kill him dead"

INSCRIPTION ON A TABLET WITH A SUSPENDED CUDGEL ON the town gate of Jüterbog, Germany

3 CYCLISTS from India

—ADI B. HAKIM, JAL P. BAPASOLA, AND RUSTOM J. BHUMGARA— *CIRCLED THE WORLD IN A PERIOD OF 4 YEARS, 5 MONTHS, 3 DAYS* **COVERING 44,000 MILES** (Oct. 15, 1923—March 18, 1928)

THE **MAILMEN** WHO NEVER RELAXED THEIR VIGILANCE

REGISTERED MAIL IN Nyasaland ONCE WAS DELIVERED BY NATIVES WHO CARRIED IT IN BAGS THAT ENVELOPED THE HEAD —SO THEIR EYES WOULD ALWAYS BE ON IT

THE **GRAVESTONE** OF TILL EULENSPIEGEL, WHO WAS A FAMED CLOWN, SHOWS HIM DISPLAYING HIS NAME IN THE FORM OF A REBUS

AN OWL (EULE) AND A MIRROR (SPIEGEL)

St. JOSEPH'S CHURCH in Port Griffith, Pa., WAS BUILT WITH DONATIONS OF 4,500,000 PENNIES

KING GEORGE III WAS THE FIRST PRINCE OF WALES TO BECOME A FATHER DURING THE LIFE OF HIS OWN FATHER *IN A PERIOD OF 353 YEARS*

THE SPEAKER OF THE BRITISH HOUSE OF COMMONS **IS THE ONLY MEMBER FORBIDDEN TO MAKE A SPEECH**

NEWBORN INFANTS in ancient Sparta, TO HASTEN THEIR GROWING UP, WERE GIVEN THEIR FIRST BATH IN A BASIN OF WINE

MOSES and **AARON WILCOX**
(1770-1827)
of North Killingworth, Conn.,
WERE IDENTICAL TWINS,
MARRIED SISTERS,
WERE LIFELONG BUSINESS PARTNERS,
WERE STRICKEN WITH THE SAME AILMENT ON THE SAME DAY.
BOTH DIED ON SEPT. 24, 1827, **AND WERE BURIED IN THE SAME GRAVE!**
THEY FOUNDED THE TOWN OF TWINSBURG, OHIO, WHICH WAS NAMED IN THEIR HONOR

THE SCHUYLER MANSION in Schuylerville, N.Y., **WAS BUILT IN JUST 17 DAYS!**
IT WAS CONSTRUCTED BY SOLDIERS UNDER GENERAL GATES AFTER THE OLD MANSION HAD BEEN BURNED BY THE BRITISH TROOPS OF GENERAL BURGOYNE

THE UMBRELLA BIRD
GETS ITS NAME FROM THE FEATHERED CREST OVER ITS HEAD AND ALSO SPORTS A "NECKTIE" - A FEATHERED APPENDAGE THAT HANGS FROM ITS NECK

THE **PARISH CHURCH** of **BOLTON** England
IS LOCATED IN THE RUINS
OF BOLTON ABBEY WHICH
*WAS CLOSED BY KING
HENRY VIII 423 YEARS AGO*

**LEWIS
BROWN**
of Lake City, Mich.,
HIS SON,
LEWIS BROWN,
AND HIS GRANDSON,
LEWIS BROWN,
*ALL WERE ILL IN
DIFFERENT HOSPITALS
SIMULTANEOUSLY*

WOMEN in Milititsch, Yugoslavia,
IN SUMMER AS WELL AS WINTER
WEAR 9 WHITE PETTICOATS

"TIGER"
A CANNON,
IS PRESERVED
in the
Canary Islands
AS A MEMORIAL TO BRITAIN'S INABILITY
TO CAPTURE THE ISLAND OF TENERIFFE
*BECAUSE IT BLEW OFF ADMIRAL
NELSON'S RIGHT ARM* (July 25, 1797)

KIRUNA in *Sweden,*
HAS THE LARGEST LAND AREA
OF ANY CITY IN THE WORLD—
IT HAS A POPULATION OF ONLY
25,000, YET COVERS AN AREA OF
5,425 SQUARE MILES

**THE HIGHEST RESTAURANT
IN THE U.S.**
IS LOCATED ON
Ajax Hill, Aspen, Colo.,
*AT AN ALTITUDE OF
11,200 FEET*

A BLACK MOURNING CLOTH
ON THE WALL OF THE CHAMBER
OF THE GRAND COUNCIL IN VENICE
REPLACED THE PORTRAIT OF
MARIN FALIERO, A RULER OF
VENICE, *WHO WAS EXECUTED
FOR CONSPIRING TO
BECOME A DICTATOR*

HIC EST LOCVS MARINI FALETRI
DECAPITATI PRO CRIMINIBVS

A **CHAIR**
IS THE ONLY ARTICLE OF
FURNITURE USED BY THE
NOMADS OF MAURITANIA
-AND WHEN THEY TRAVEL
IT IS UPENDED AND SERVES
AS A CAMEL SADDLE
*THE YOUNG WOMEN RIDE
THE CAMELS AND THE OLD
WOMEN WALK*

Sea Coral

FOUND in the Northern Andes Mountains of Chile AT A HEIGHT OF 17,000 FEET

THE MOUNTAINS ONCE WERE BELOW SEA LEVEL

A SAVAGE STALLION

AS PUNISHMENT FOR KILLING A MAN, WAS FORCED BY KING NASIR-UD-DIN OF OUDH, INDIA, TO FIGHT A CAPTIVE TIGER

—BUT THE HORSE KILLED THE TIGER (1849)

GERARD de NERVAL

1808 - 1855

CELEBRATED FRENCH POET, FOR YEARS TOOK A DAILY WALK IN THE PARKS OF PARIS

LEADING A LIVE LOBSTER ON A LEASH

THE **ECHIDNA** AN EGG-LAYING ANIMAL HAS HIND FEET THAT TURN BACKWARD

RUBBER BALL WITH BERMUDA GRASS GROWING THROUGH IT

CHRISTOPHER **COLUMBUS** SAVED HIS LIFE BY ADVANCE KNOWLEDGE OF A **LUNAR ECLIPSE!**

HIS ALMANAC ENABLED HIM TO COW REBELLIOUS NATIVES AT ST. ANN'S BAY, JAMAICA, IN 1504

A **SILVER OYSTER SHELL** WAS USED IN Colchester, England, AS A BASIS OF COMPARISON TO MAKE SURE NO UNDERSIZED OYSTERS WERE MARKETED

FOOD

THE **TARSIER** A LIVING FOSSIL HAS EXISTED FOR 70,000,000 YEARS

THE CHURCH of PAPARDURA in Enna, Sicily, WAS BUILT *INSIDE A MOUNTAIN CAVE* (1546)

THE OCEAN LIGHTS

LUMINOUS JELLYFISH (Pelagia Noctiluca) SHED SUCH BRILLIANT LIGHT, THAT TRAVELING IN CLUSTERS, *THEY LIGHT UP THE DARK OCEAN FOR MILES*

THE NIGHTINGALE SINGS DURING ITS NESTING PERIOD TO *WARN OFF INTRUDERS*

JOHN G. GUILFORD of Palatka, Fla., BOWLED 9 SUCCESSIVE STRIKES —YET HE IS *TOTALLY BLIND !*

THE BLURRED CASTLE THE CASTLE of SASSOCORVARO, Italy, WAS BUILT WITH WAVY OUTLINES IN 1475 BECAUSE THE PLANS BROUGHT TEARS OF EMOTION TO THE EYES OF COUNT UBALDINI di URBINO *AND HE ORDERED THAT THE FINISHED STRUCTURE SHOULD ALSO APPEAR BLURRED*

BEN and ELINORE CARLIN
A HUSBAND AND WIFE
CROSSED THE ATLANTIC IN 1950
IN AN AMPHIBIOUS JEEP
THEY SAILED FROM HALIFAX, N.S.,
TO THE AZORES, TRAVELING
1,800 MILES IN 31 DAYS

ANTOINE-EUGÈNE SCRIBE
(1791-1861) French playwright
WROTE 7 PLAYS EACH YEAR
FOR 50 SUCCESSIVE YEARS

THE **4TH EARL of PERTH**
1648-1716
WHO AS LORD CHANCELLOR OF SCOTLAND WAS HIS COUNTRY'S HIGHEST JUDICIAL OFFICER, SEVERAL TIMES PRESIDED AT TRIALS IN WHICH HE WAS BOTH JUDGE **AND DEFENDANT!**

EACH TIME HE DECIDED IN HIS OWN FAVOR

TRAILS in Ethiopia **ARE MARKED BY TYING YOUNG TREES IN KNOTS**

MARIO MASINI
A WAITER IN PRATO, ITALY, IN THE 19th CENTURY
MEMORIZED ALL THE WORKS OF DANTE
A TOTAL OF MORE THAN 300,000 WORDS

GURNAH, a modern village, WAS BUILT BY THE EGYPTIAN GOVERNMENT FAR FROM the Valley of Kings
SO RESIDENTS OF THE OLD COMMUNITY WOULD NO LONGER BE ABLE TO **LOOT THE TOMBS OF THE KINGS**
–BUT THE NATIVES REFUSED TO MOVE – AND THE NEW VILLAGE REMAINS A GHOST COMMUNITY

YOUNG PELICANS CRAWL INSIDE THEIR MOTHER'S BILL AND EAT DIRECTLY FROM HER CROP

THE **NEST** OF THE MASON BEE IS CONSTRUCTED INSIDE THE WHORLS OF *AN ABANDONED SNAIL SHELL*

THE **MOSQUE** of the Oasis of Gicherra, in Cyrenaica, Africa, CONSTRUCTED OF PALM LEAVES, *IN THE LAST 160 YEARS HAS BEEN COMPLETELY REBUILT 480 TIMES!*

YAKCOWS of Mongolia *OFFSPRING OF A YAK AND A COW*

Penelope SMITH of County Cork, Ireland, WAS SO PROUD OF LANDING the Prince of Capua, Italy, AS HER HUSBAND THAT SHE *MARRIED HIM 4 TIMES* TO ONE OF THE CEREMONIES SHE INVITED 13 SUITORS SHE HAD REJECTED (1836)

A **MEMORIAL** ERECTED IN THE Southern Vosges Mountains of France TO HEROIC MEMBERS OF MINE DISPOSAL SQUADS OF WORLD WAR II *DEPICTS THE PREMATURE EXPLOSION OF A ROAD MINE WITH A SOLDIER BEING HURTLED TO HIS DEATH*

NIUMAN KOPROLI

ONE OF THE MOST FAMED GRAND VIZIERS IN TURKISH HISTORY BECAME CONVINCED THAT HE HAD A FLY BUZZING INSIDE HIS NOSE — DR. LEDUC OF FRANCE PALMED A DEAD FLY, TOLD THE GRAND VIZIER IT HAD BEEN REMOVED BY SURGERY — AND KOPROLI NEVER AGAIN WAS TROUBLED BY HIS STRANGE MALADY (1710)

A **COMET** SIGHTED IN 1744 HAD **6 TAILS**

THE **DUCK HAWK** "CUTS" ITS MEAT WITH THE AID OF A SINGLE SHARP TOOTH IN ITS BEAK

THE LINCOLN SPIRE of Christ Church, in Lambeth, England, IS PRESERVED AS A MEMORIAL TO THE AMERICAN PRESIDENT AS PART OF A MODERN OFFICE BUILDING — GERMAN BOMBS IN WORLD WAR II DESTROYED THE CHURCH — **BUT THE SPIRE REMAINED UNHARMED**

A **RING PUZZLE** CREATED BY A CHINESE HERO NAMED HUNG-MING IN 211 TO KEEP HIS WIFE FROM BEING BORED WHILE HE WAS AWAY *BECAME THE GIFT ALL CHINESE WARRIORS PRESENTED TO THEIR WIVES FOR CENTURIES*

THE **DOOR KNOCKER** of Durham Cathedral, England, IS SHAPED LIKE A CAT'S HEAD AND WHEN THE SCREW IN EACH EYE IS MOVED, IT *CHANGES FROM A SMILING WELCOME TO A SCOWL*

THE **GREAT TEMPLE of RUANWELLI** in Anuradhapura, Ceylon, 155 FEET HIGH AND 900 FEET IN CIRCUMFERENCE, WAS BUILT BY KING DUTTA GAMINI WITHOUT MORTAR *- YET IT HAS ENDURED FOR 2,100 YEARS*

A **TABLE FAN** OPERATED BY A SPRING THAT WAS WOUND WITH A KEY WAS POPULAR IN 19TH-CENTURY AMERICAN HOMES TO *DRIVE AWAY FLIES AND MOSQUITOES*

CHARLES WESLEY (1709-1788) of London, England, COMPOSED 6,500 HYMNS *-MOST OF THEM ON HORSEBACK*

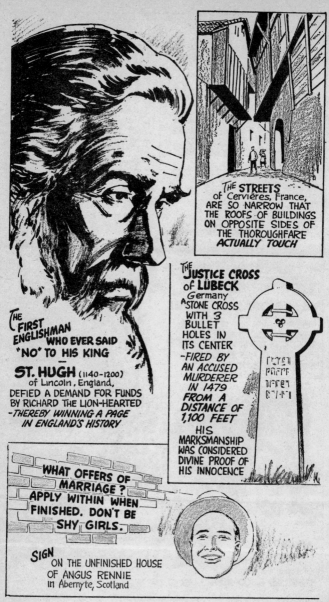

THE STREETS of Cervières, France, ARE SO NARROW THAT THE ROOFS OF BUILDINGS ON OPPOSITE SIDES OF THE THOROUGHFARE *ACTUALLY TOUCH*

THE FIRST ENGLISHMAN WHO EVER SAID "NO" TO HIS KING —

ST. HUGH (1140-1200) of Lincoln, England, DEFIED A DEMAND FOR FUNDS BY RICHARD THE LION-HEARTED —*THEREBY WINNING A PAGE IN ENGLAND'S HISTORY*

THE JUSTICE CROSS of LÜBECK Germany A STONE CROSS WITH 3 BULLET HOLES IN ITS CENTER —FIRED BY AN ACCUSED MURDERER IN 1479 FROM A DISTANCE OF 1,100 FEET

HIS MARKSMANSHIP WAS CONSIDERED DIVINE PROOF OF HIS INNOCENCE

WHAT OFFERS OF MARRIAGE? APPLY WITHIN WHEN FINISHED. DON'T BE SHY GIRLS.

SIGN ON THE UNFINISHED HOUSE OF ANGUS RENNIE in Abernyte, Scotland

MRS. **LENORA WHEELER** of Jonesport, Maine, GAVE EACH OF HER 5 DAUGHTERS **THE SAME INITIALS**

JOAN **E**LAINE **W**HEELER
JANICE **E**TTA **W**HEELER
JOYCE **E**ILEEN **W**HEELER
JEAN **E**VELYN **W**HEELER
JUDITH **E**ONE **W**HEELER

A **TIN CROCODILE** WAS A COIN IN THE 17TH CENTURY ON THE MALAY PENINSULA

THE **MAN** WHOSE MEMORIAL IS REPRINTED EVERY DAY

FRANCESCO PETRARCA (1304-1374) THE FAMED ITALIAN POET WAS MEMORIALIZED BY THE 15th-CENTURY PRINTER, MANUZIO, WHO CREATED THE TYPE KNOWN AS ITALIC BY COPYING PETRARCA'S SLANTING HANDWRITING

KARL DEWEY MYERS (1899-1951) who became Poet Laureate of West Virginia WAS A CRIPPLE WHO NEVER WEIGHED MORE THAN 60 POUNDS AND **WAS COMPLETELY SELF-EDUCATED**

HE MEMORIZED THE DECLARATION OF INDEPENDENCE, THE CONSTITUTION OF THE U.S., THE MAYFLOWER COMPACT AND THE MAGNA CHARTA

109

3 FRIENDS
of Sooss, Austria,
KARL GANNESHOFER, WHO
LIVED TO BE 82 -HIS BROTHER,
FRANZ, WHO DIED AT 78-
AND FRANZ BRENDINGER,
WHO LIVED 77 YEARS-
DRANK DURING THEIR
LIFETIMES A TOTAL OF
149,354 QUARTS OF
HOMEMADE WINE

ST. PAUL'S CHURCH
in Damascus, Syria,
WAS BUILT OVER THE ANCIENT
CITY WALL SO THAT THE
CITY GATE SERVES AS
ENTRYWAY TO THE CHURCH

DR. JACOB SCHAEFFER
of Germany
MANUFACTURED PAPER IN 1770
FROM 90 DIFFERENT TYPES
OF PLANTS - INCLUDING-
HOPS AND POTATOES

A WATER SURVEY in Elgin, Texas, IS BEING CONDUCTED BY FRANK T. DROUGHT

THE CHURCH of the "TWIN TOWERS"

THE CHURCH OF FJENNESLEVLILLE
Denmark
WAS BUILT BY ASGER RIG, WHO, LEAVING FOR WAR BEFORE ITS COMPLETION AND WHILE HIS WIFE WAS EXPECTING A CHILD, ORDERED A SPIRE CONSTRUCTED IF THE INFANT WAS A GIRL — AND A TOWER IF IT WAS A BOY

ASGER'S FIRST GLIMPSE OF HIS TOWN ON HIS RETURN REVEALED HE HAD BECOME THE FATHER OF TWIN BOYS

ROQUE ANSOLA (1824-1913) A DRUMMER, PLAYED CLASSICAL MUSIC IN THE PLAZA OF ELGOIBAR, Spain, *EVERY MORNING FOR 69 YEARS*

THE GREAT KAWIR DESERT in Persia IS COVERED WITH A WHITE SALT CRUST SO TREACHEROUS THAT MANY TRAVELERS HAVE PERISHED BY FALLING THROUGH IT *INTO AN APPARENTLY BOTTOMLESS MORASS*

WINE DRINKERS in Zurich, Switzerland, WITH AN INTELLECTUAL BENT, IMBIBED IN THE 16th CENTURY *FROM CUPS SHAPED LIKE BOOKS*

KING ALARIC

OF THE VISIGOTHS WAS BURIED IN 410 IN THE BED OF THE BUSENTO RIVER, IN COSENZA, ITALY, MOUNTED ON HIS FAVORITE CHARGER *--THE RIVER BEING DIVERTED DURING THE INTERMENT* THE SLAVES WHO HELPED SHIFT THE RIVER WERE SLAIN TO KEEP HIS FINAL RESTING PLACE A SECRET FOREVER

THE LARGE-MOUTH BLACK BASS IS KNOWN BY *44 DIFFERENT NAMES*

MICHEL MUSSON OF NEW ORLEANS, LA., A FRIEND OF PRESIDENT ZACHARY TAYLOR, *REJECTED THE OFFICE OF POSTMASTER GENERAL OF THE U.S. IN 1849--BECOMING, INSTEAD, POSTMASTER OF NEW ORLEANS*

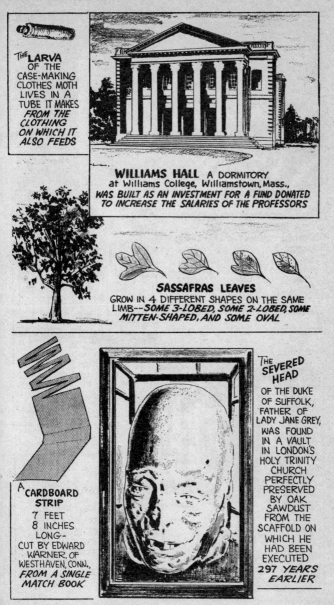

THE LARVA OF THE CASE-MAKING CLOTHES MOTH LIVES IN A TUBE IT MAKES *FROM THE CLOTHING ON WHICH IT ALSO FEEDS*

WILLIAMS HALL A DORMITORY
at Williams College, Williamstown, Mass.,
WAS BUILT AS AN INVESTMENT FOR A FUND DONATED TO INCREASE THE SALARIES OF THE PROFESSORS

SASSAFRAS LEAVES
GROW IN 4 DIFFERENT SHAPES ON THE SAME LIMB-- *SOME 3-LOBED, SOME 2-LOBED, SOME MITTEN-SHAPED, AND SOME OVAL*

A **CARDBOARD STRIP** 7 FEET 8 INCHES LONG-CUT BY EDWARD WARNER, OF WESTHAVEN, CONN., *FROM A SINGLE MATCH BOOK*

THE SEVERED HEAD OF THE DUKE OF SUFFOLK, FATHER OF LADY JANE GREY, WAS FOUND IN A VAULT IN LONDON'S HOLY TRINITY CHURCH PERFECTLY PRESERVED BY OAK SAWDUST FROM THE SCAFFOLD ON WHICH HE HAD BEEN EXECUTED *297 YEARS EARLIER*

THE PROPHECY THAT FRIGHTENED A MAN TO DEATH

CARDINAL THOMAS WOLSEY (1475-1530) WARNED BY A FORTUNE-TELLER THAT KINGSTON WOULD MARK THE END OF HIS LIFE, AVOIDED THE TOWN OF THAT NAME FOR YEARS, *BUT WHEN KING HENRY VIII SENT A CONSTABLE NAMED KINGSTON AFTER WOLSEY, HE DIED OF SHOCK*

ST. ANDREW'S TOWER

IN Peebles, Scotland, IS THE ONLY REMAINING PART OF A CHURCH THAT *WAS TWICE DESTROYED BY INVADING ARMIES*

THE BALANCING BOULDER

A HUGE ROCK, HUELGOAT, FRANCE, 23 FEET LONG AND 16 FEET WIDE --YET SO DELICATELY BALANCED THAT A CHILD COULD TEETER IT

THE TUFTED BEETLE

IS SHELTERED AND FED BY ANTS IN THEIR NEST BECAUSE IT EXUDES A TYPE OF HONEY --ALTHOUGH AS PART OF ITS FOOD IT EATS *THE ANTS' LARVAE*

THE STAMP THAT COST 15,000 LIVES!

A SANTO DOMINGO STAMP ISSUED IN 1900, BECAUSE IT SHOWED THAT COUNTRY'S BORDER EXTENDING INTO HAITI, TOUCHED OFF CONFLICTS THAT CONTINUED FOR 38 YEARS AND *CLAIMED 15,000 LIVES*

THE KABANGS

BOATS USED BY THE MAWKEN NATIVES OF THE SO. CHINA SEA -- WHO SPEND THEIR ENTIRE LIVES AT SEA -- ARE MADE UNSINKABLE BY ENCASING THE HULLS WITH *TWISTED PALM LEAF STEMS*

THE SOLDIER WHO WAS MADE A FAMOUS AUTHOR BY A DUEL

XAVIER de MAISTRE (1763-1852) JAILED IN ALESSANDRIA, ITALY, FOR FIGHTING A DUEL, BECAME SO BORED THAT HE WROTE A DESCRIPTION OF HIS CELL ENTITLED:
"A TRIP AROUND MY CHAMBER"
IT BECAME SUCH A SUCCESS THAT IT MADE THE HUMBLE SOLDIER A CELEBRATED FRENCH AUTHOR

HERE LIES
ONE FOOTE, WHOSE DEATH
MAY THOUSANDS SAVE
FOR DEATH
HAS NOW ONE FOOTE
WITHIN THE GRAVE

EPITAPH of SAMUEL FOOTE ENGLISH DRAMATIST AND ACTOR IN WESTMINSTER ABBEY, LONDON, ENGLAND

Never Hit Your Mother
With a Shovel
It Leaves a Very Bad
Impression on Her Mind

NAME OF A STUDIO
LISTED IN THE LOS ANGELES,
CALIF., PHONE DIRECTORY

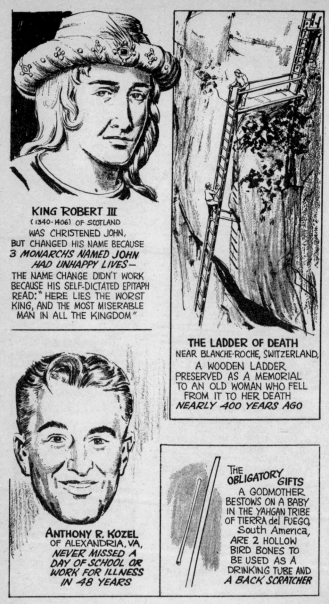

KING ROBERT III
(1340-1406) OF SCOTLAND
WAS CHRISTENED JOHN,
BUT CHANGED HIS NAME BECAUSE
*3 MONARCHS NAMED JOHN
HAD UNHAPPY LIVES—*
THE NAME CHANGE DIDN'T WORK
BECAUSE HIS SELF-DICTATED EPITAPH
READ:" HERE LIES THE WORST
KING, AND THE MOST MISERABLE
MAN IN ALL THE KINGDOM "

THE LADDER OF DEATH
NEAR BLANCHE-ROCHE, SWITZERLAND,
A WOODEN LADDER
PRESERVED AS A MEMORIAL
TO AN OLD WOMAN WHO FELL
FROM IT TO HER DEATH
NEARLY 400 YEARS AGO

ANTHONY R. KOZEL
OF ALEXANDRIA, VA,
*NEVER MISSED A
DAY OF SCHOOL OR
WORK FOR ILLNESS
IN 48 YEARS*

THE
OBLIGATORY GIFTS
A GODMOTHER
BESTOWS ON A BABY
IN THE YAHGAN TRIBE
OF TIERRA del FUEGO,
South America,
ARE 2 HOLLOW
BIRD BONES TO
BE USED AS A
DRINKING TUBE AND
A BACK SCRATCHER

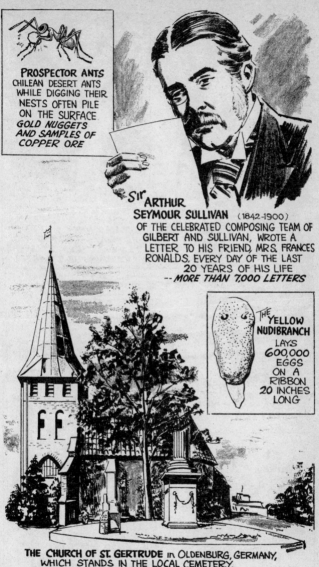

PROSPECTOR ANTS CHILEAN DESERT ANTS WHILE DIGGING THEIR NESTS OFTEN PILE ON THE SURFACE *GOLD NUGGETS AND SAMPLES OF COPPER ORE*

SIR ARTHUR SEYMOUR SULLIVAN (1842-1900) OF THE CELEBRATED COMPOSING TEAM OF GILBERT AND SULLIVAN, WROTE A LETTER TO HIS FRIEND, MRS. FRANCES RONALDS, EVERY DAY OF THE LAST 20 YEARS OF HIS LIFE -- *MORE THAN 7,000 LETTERS*

THE **YELLOW NUDIBRANCH** LAYS 600,000 EGGS ON A RIBBON 20 INCHES LONG

THE **CHURCH OF ST. GERTRUDE** in OLDENBURG, GERMANY, WHICH STANDS IN THE LOCAL CEMETERY, BEARS OVER ITS ENTRANCE THE INSCRIPTION: *"O forever is such a long time"*

THE BOULDER BRIDGE, France
A NATURAL BRIDGE OVER THE NÉRON RIVER, NEAR GRENOBLE, *CREATED WHEN A GIGANTIC ROCK WAS DROPPED INTO PLACE BETWEEN 2 CLIFFS DURING THE ICE AGE*

TARAHUMARE INDIANS
OF MEXICO
SHOOT FISH WITH A
MINIATURE BOW AND ARROWS

I'D RATHER HAVE MAN'S KNUCKLES.

THE PIG THAT ATE LIKE A MAN
GRIMOD de la REYNIÈRE
(1758-1838)
A FRENCH GOURMET
*TRAINED A PET PIG
TO DINE REGULARLY
AT HIS TABLE*

THIS ENTRANCE
TO THE CATHEDRAL OF ST. SIFFREIN,
IN CARPENTRAS, FRANCE,
IS CALLED LA PORTE JUIVE
BECAUSE IT WAS BUILT IN
THE MIDDLE AGES WITH
DONATIONS FROM THE
CITY'S JEWISH COMMUNITY

THE **TRIPLE BLOOMS** OF THE GREATER FLEABANE—EACH BLOOM CONSISTS OF AS MANY *AS 700 COMPLETE FLOWERS*

THOMAS JEFFERSON INTRODUCED THE U.S. *TO ICE CREAM*—HE PURCHASED AN ICE CREAM MACHINE IN FRANCE IN 1789

COUNT SUWOROW (1729-1800) A FIELD MARSHAL OF OLD RUSSIA SERVED AS HIS OWN "BUGLER"—*AWAKENING HIS TROOPS EACH MORNING BY CROWING LIKE A ROOSTER*

MARGARITA STABBED BY GOLD DOLLAR

EPITAPH IN BOOTHILL CEMETERY, Tombstone, Ariz.

KING IBN SAUD (1880-1953) of Saudi Arabia WAS MARRIED **400** TIMES

-YET NEVER SAW THE FACE OF ANY OF HIS BRIDES BEFORE HE MARRIED HER

A **CANCELLED BANK CHECK** OWNED BY MRS. ELTA STODDARD WAS BLOWN BY A TORNADO FROM HER HOME IN Manitou Beach, Michigan, ACROSS LAKE ST. CLAIR TO Alvinston, Ontario, **A DISTANCE OF 175 MILES** IT WAS FOUND ON THE FARM OF WILLIAM CAMPBELL IN ALVINSTON AND RETURNED BY MAIL April 11, 1965

ROBERT LANGNEY AN ENGLISHMAN living in Paris, France, *TRANSCRIBED THE ENTIRE BIBLE FROM MEMORY* HIS WORK, WHICH REQUIRED 3 YEARS, WAS FOUND TO CONTAIN ONLY 11 MINOR ERRORS

THE **SERIEMA** A BIRD of Paraguay and Brazil **BARKS LIKE A DOG**

THE HARNESS ANTELOPE
Tragelaphus scriptus
HAS THE MARKINGS OF A
HARNESS ON ITS BACK

DUKE LORENZO THE MAGNIFICENT
(1449-1492) The ruler of Florence
IN THE LAST WEEK OF
A FATAL ILLNESS, WAS
**ADMINISTERED $250,000
WORTH OF MEDICINE**

*HIS PHYSICIAN, PIER LEONI,
FED HIM WINE INTO WHICH
HAD BEEN GROUND PEARLS,
RUBIES AND DIAMONDS!*

JOSEPH BARKER
FOR THREATENING TO LYNCH
JUDGE BENJAMIN PATTON,
WAS SENTENCED TO A YEAR
IN JAIL BY JUDGE PATTON
-YET HE WAS ELECTED
MAYOR OF PITTSBURGH, PA.,
WHILE IN PRISON AND WAS
*SWORN INTO OFFICE BY
JUDGE PATTON* (1849-50)

A BRONZE MORTAR
in Hildesheim, Germany,
WEIGHING 258½ LBS.,
HAS BEEN USED
FOR THE POUNDING
OF PRESCRIPTIONS
IN THE SAME
DRUGSTORE
SINCE 1723

A **BRIDGE** SPANNING A CANAL IN THE SUNDARBANS DISTRICT OF INDIA --*MADE FROM BUNDLES OF BAMBOO BY ONE MAN IN A SINGLE AFTERNOON*

THE INDIAN FORT THEATRE
near Berea, Kentucky,
WAS BUILT ENTIRELY WITH ROCKS SALVAGED FROM OLD STONE FENCES IN THE AREA

DR. GASPARD LEONARD SCRIVE
(1815-1861) Chief Military Surgeon of the French Army
WAS DECORATED DURING THE CRIMEAN WAR BY THE ENEMY !
THE RUSSIAN GOVERNMENT AWARDED DR. SCRIVE THE ORDER OF ST. STANISLAS FOR HUMANITY TOWARD PRISONERS OF WAR

DANTE'S ROCK
Cape Manerba, Italy
NATURAL PROFILE OF
THE ITALIAN POET

ISKANDER BEG
TO BRING NEWS OF THE DEATH OF SHAH ISMAIL II
OF PERSIA, RODE THE SAME HORSE DAY AND
NIGHT FROM KAZWIN TO SHIRAZ
—COVERING 620 MILES IN 6 DAYS
HE WAS JAILED IN THE BELIEF HE WAS A SPY
SENT TO TEST THE LOYALTY OF ISMAIL'S HEIR
—AND THE HORSE DIED

A **BATHTUB** delivered to the Pitti Palace
in Florence, Italy, in 1458 AND
TEMPORARILY PLACED IN THE COURTYARD
TO AWAIT COMPLETION OF THE PALACE, IS
STILL IN THE YARD 507 YEARS LATER

**MANGABEY
MONKEYS**
SHOW THE WHITES
OF THEIR EYES
ONLY WHEN THEIR
EYES ARE CLOSED
THEIR EYELIDS ARE
A GHOSTLY WHITE

123

Count CHRISTOPH SCHWERIN
1684 - 1757
FAMED PRUSSIAN ARMY OFFICER, ALL HIS LIFE EXPRESSED THE WISH **THAT HE DIE BY A CANNON BALL OR BE HANGED AT THE AGE OF 80—** *HE WAS KILLED BY A CANNON BALL IN THE BATTLE OF PRAGUE (May 6, 1757)*

THE GRAVE OF THE BIBLICAL PATRIARCH, ABRAHAM, in Hebron, Jordan, IS GUARDED BY A GRILL MADE OF **SOLID SILVER**

THE **ROYAL PALACE of ACHIN** in Sumatra WAS BUILT AROUND A GIANT SACRED TREE *SO THE ENTIRE STRUCTURE WOULD BENEFIT FROM* **ITS REVERED SHADE**

FEMALE MARINE FIREWORMS RISE TO THE SURFACE OF THE SEA AT NIGHT *AND TURN ON THEIR LIGHTS TO ATTRACT A MATE*

HERE LIES
ANDREW
MACPHERSON
WHO WAS A
PECULIAR PERSON
HE STOOD
SIX FEET TWO
WITHOUT HIS SHOE
AND HE WAS SLEW
AT WATERLOO

Epitaph in
Dumfries Churchyard,
Scotland

MICHELANGELO
AFTER WORKING FROM A
SCAFFOLD IN THE SISTINE CHAPEL
FOR **6 YEARS** WITH HIS ARMS
RAISED AND HIS HEAD TILTED
BACK, COULD READ ONLY WHAT
WAS HELD ABOVE HIS HEAD

TUAREG MEN
of N. Africa

ARE
FORBIDDEN
TO REMOVE
THEIR
VEILS IN
PUBLIC
-AND CANNOT
WED UNTIL
**A GIRL HAS
PROPOSED
MARRIAGE**

*THE
GROOM
CHOSEN
MUST
BRING A
DOWRY OF
7 CAMELS*

A **PIGEON'S
NEST**
CONSTRUCTED
ON A SILL
in Buenos Aires,
Argentina,
**ENTIRELY
OF NAILS**
(1959)

125

THE **MELODY** OF THE NATIONAL ANTHEM OF TIBET IS THE SAME AS THAT OF **"AMERICA"**

THE **BRIDGE THAT WAS HONORABLY RETIRED**

The Bridge of Tiberius in Rimini, Italy, AFTER BEING USED FOR 1,941 YEARS HAS BEEN OFFICIALLY CLOSED -**BUT IS STILL LEFT STANDING AS ITS OWN MEMORIAL**

BOYS IN THE THOUSANDS OF RIVERBOAT FAMILIES OF Canton, China, ARE PROTECTED FROM DROWNING *BY* **BAMBOO LIFEBELTS**- GIRLS ARE NOT CONSIDERED VALUABLE ENOUGH TO SAFEGUARD

SKIS ARE USED BY NOMAD LAPPS OF Northern Europe AS **GRAVE MARKERS**

THE CHURCH WITH NO FAÇADE

The Church of Santa Maria degli Angeli, in Rome, Italy, WAS BUILT INSIDE THE RUINS OF THE PUBLIC BATHS ORIGINALLY CONSTRUCTED BY EMPEROR DIOCLETIAN *1,660 YEARS AGO*

THE BRIDGE OVER

the Goldbrook River, in Hoxne, England, HAS NOT BEEN USED BY BRIDAL PARTIES *FOR 1,092 YEARS*

KING EDMUND OF EAST ANGLIA PUT A CURSE ON ALL BRIDES AND GROOMS WHO MIGHT USE THE BRIDGE AFTER HE WAS BETRAYED TO THE DANES BY A WEDDING PARTY THAT SPOTTED HIM *HIDING BENEATH IT IN THE YEAR 870*

HUNTERS

IN EUROPE IN THE 17TH AND 18TH CENTURIES CREPT UP ON THEIR PREY BY CONCEALING THEMSELVES *IN PORTABLE TREES*

THE **ENTIRE VILLAGE OF GUKUNG** in Tibet CONSISTING OF SEVERAL HUNDRED PERSONS, THEIR HOMES AND LIVESTOCK *IS LOCATED INSIDE A CAVE*

JOHANN GEORG KRÜNITZ

(1728 - 1796)
of Germany
WROTE AN ENCYCLOPEDIA
OF **242** VOLUMES
ALL IN LONGHAND!
*HE ALSO TURNED OUT **438** OTHER LARGE BOOKS*

RAFAEL CARRERA
(1814-1865)
WAS ELECTED A LIFETIME
PRESIDENT OF GUATEMALA
*BEFORE HE HAD LEARNED
TO WRITE HIS OWN NAME*

THE **LARGE LEAF WORM** WHICH IS ALMOST ROUND, HAS 100 EYES SENSITIVE TO LIGHT -YET IT CANNOT SEE OBJECTS IN ITS PATH.

THE **HOTEL des RUINES**
in Villers-la-ville, France,
A MODERN HOSTELRY
*IS LOCATED IN THE RUINS
OF A 12th CENTURY ABBEY*

THE **MOST MODEST PAINTER
IN ALL HISTORY**

Jan Klaas Rietschoof
(1652 - 1719)
LEADING DUTCH MARINE
PAINTER OF HIS TIME,
NEVER PUT A PRICE ON
ANY OF HIS WORK AND
WHEN ANYONE MADE AN
OFFER FOR A PAINTING
*-ALWAYS SOLD IT
FOR 50% LESS*

ADRIEN BARON PLANCY
(1778-1855) HAVING WON $189,140
PLAYING BACCARAT IN A CLUB
IN PARIS, FRANCE,
WAS ABOUT TO CASH IN HIS
WINNINGS, BUT DECIDED TO
TRY FOR ANOTHER $3,660
--AN EVEN MILLION FRANCS
HE LOST EVERYTHING HE HAD WON

THE **TOUCAN**
AFTER EACH MEAL
*CAREFULLY WIPES ITS
BILL ON A TREE BRANCH*

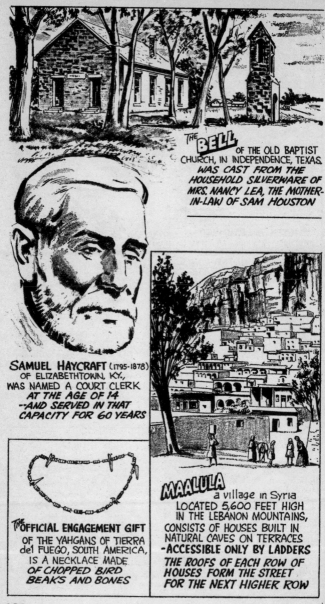

THE **BELL** OF THE OLD BAPTIST CHURCH, IN INDEPENDENCE, TEXAS, *WAS CAST FROM THE HOUSEHOLD SILVERWARE OF MRS. NANCY LEA, THE MOTHER-IN-LAW OF SAM HOUSTON*

SAMUEL HAYCRAFT (1795-1878) OF ELIZABETHTOWN, KY., WAS NAMED A COURT CLERK *AT THE AGE OF 14 --AND SERVED IN THAT CAPACITY FOR 60 YEARS*

THE **OFFICIAL ENGAGEMENT GIFT** OF THE YAHGANS OF TIERRA del FUEGO, SOUTH AMERICA, IS A NECKLACE MADE *OF CHOPPED BIRD BEAKS AND BONES*

MAALULA a village in Syria LOCATED 5,600 FEET HIGH IN THE LEBANON MOUNTAINS, CONSISTS OF HOUSES BUILT IN NATURAL CAVES ON TERRACES -ACCESSIBLE ONLY BY LADDERS *THE ROOFS OF EACH ROW OF HOUSES FORM THE STREET FOR THE NEXT HIGHER ROW*

YOUNG ABORIGINES OF CENTRAL AUSTRALIA PLEAT THE HAIRS OF THEIR BEARD AROUND *THE CURVED TAIL OF A THALGOO -- AN AUSTRALIAN MAMMAL*

A STURGEON LAYS AS MANY AS 5,000,000 EGGS AT ONE TIME THE EGGS WEIGH AS MUCH AS 55 POUNDS

THE PRETTIEST SCARECROWS IN THE WORLD!
SCARECROWS CONSTRUCTED BY DUTCH FARMERS OFTEN ARE *LIFESIZE LIKENESSES OF THEIR WIVES OR DAUGHTERS*

THE BELFRY of the CATHEDRAL OF ST. THEODORIT, in Uzes, France, *IS THE ONLY ROUND CHURCH TOWER IN ALL FRANCE*

COUNT ALEXIS BESTUZHEV-RIUMIN
(1695-1766) of Russia
A DIPLOMAT FOR HALF A CENTURY, ROSE TO BECOME CHANCELLOR OF THE RUSSIAN EMPIRE *BECAUSE HE MUMBLED SO BADLY HE COULD ALWAYS CLAIM HE HAD BEEN MISUNDERSTOOD*

A **ROMAN CALENDAR** in the SHAPE OF A CUBE FOUND IN THE ASHES OF POMPEII

LOMÉNIE de BRIENNE
(1635- 1698)
BECAME FRENCH SECRETARY OF FOREIGN AFFAIRS, THE HIGHEST DIPLOMATIC POST IN HIS COUNTRY *WHEN HE WAS ONLY 16 YEARS OF AGE*

THE **GRAVE** OF A NATIVE CHIEF of Madagascar IS ADORNED BY A PAIR OF HORNS *FOR EACH YEAR OF HIS REIGN*

REES LEWIS
(1797-1884)
A FAMED SEA CAPTAIN
of Aberdowy, Wales,
WAS THE FATHER OF
3 SHIP CAPTAINS
*AND ALL 3 OF HIS DAUGHTERS
MARRIED SEA CAPTAINS*

THE CONSCIENTIOUS PRISONER
A **SPY** ARRESTED BY CONSTABLE
JOSEPH ROSENVINGE
of Ribe, Denmark,
*WAS LEFT ALONE WHILE HIS
CAPTOR WENT TO LUNCH*
—AND FAITHFULLY GUARDED
THE CONSTABLE'S RIFLE
1848

133

AN AVALANCHE OF HUGE BOULDERS

ROLLING DOWN MT. CALANDA IN 1844 SENT THE INHABITANTS OF FELSBERG, SWITZERLAND, INTO FLIGHT - *BUT THE ROCKS HALTED HALFWAY DOWN THE SLOPE*

MAXIMILIAN I
(1573-1651) of Bavaria

WAS THE ONLY ONE OF GERMANY'S 300 RULERS AND PRINCES WHO KEPT HIS THRONE THROUGHOUT THE ENTIRE 30 YEARS' WAR

PROFESSOR JOHANN SCHROEDER
(1680-1756)

NAMED EACH OF HIS 4 SONS AFTER A GERMAN OR DUTCH UNIVERSITY - *AND EACH BECAME A PROFESSOR AT THE UNIVERSITY AFTER WHICH HE WAS NAMED*

SIAMESE TWIN MOUTH-BREEDING FISH
(Tilapia macrocephala)
THE FEMALE BREEDS ITS YOUNG IN ITS MOUTH

134

LAST LAUGH!

DONALD McDONALD
A HIGHWAYMAN OF BOHUNTIN, SCOTLAND, SENTENCED BY LORD SEAFIELD TO BE HANGED, ASKED TO BE BEHEADED INSTEAD BECAUSE HE WANTED TO SPITE THE JUDGE, WHO HAD SAID:
"I'LL SEE YOU HANGED, IF IT'S THE LAST THING I DO"

RANDELL JORDAN
of Winnfield, La.,
WAS SHOT THROUGH THE FOREHEAD WHILE HUNTING, STOPPED BREATHING ON THE OPERATING TABLE, AND STILL CARRIES THE BUCKSHOT IN HIS HEAD
-YET HE HAS COMPLETELY RECOVERED

from an old print

A **GUILLOTINE**
WAS USED BY THE IRISH *NEARLY 500 YEARS BEFORE IT WAS ADOPTED BY THE FRENCH* AN OLD PRINT PORTRAYS AN EXECUTION IN MERTON, IRELAND, ON APRIL 1, 1307

135

THE PALACE OF THE **TURKISH GOVERNOR** in Riadh, capital of Saudi Arabia, TO DEMONSTRATE THE PRESENT GOVERNMENT'S SCORN FOR THE TURKS, *WAS CONVERTED INTO A PRISON*

THE BELFRY THAT'S 150 MILES FROM ITS TEMPLE! Kalgan, Mongolia.

IN 1420 EMPEROR YUNG LOH ORDERED A GIGANTIC TEMPLE HONORING HIS ANCESTORS-- **TO REACH FROM KALGAN TO PEIPING** *WORK WAS STARTED AT BOTH ENDS OF THE TEMPLE -- BUT THE PROJECT WAS NEVER FINISHED*

SAMUEL THURSTON of Whitesboro, N.Y., FOR A PERIOD OF **9** YEARS (1794-1803) HEARD THE REV. BETHUEL DODD DELIVER THE SAME SERMON ON ALTERNATE SUNDAYS IN WHITESBORO AND UTICA *-RIDING HORSEBACK A TOTAL OF 40 MILES TO HEAR IT THE SECOND TIME*

CAPT. J.B. BROOKS
PILOTING HIS
TUGBOAT "ARDITCH"
off Snohomish County,
Washington, in Oct., 1915,
WITH MRS. ELIDA EVANS, A
PASSENGER, THE ONLY
OTHER PERSON ABOARD
**VANISHED SUDDENLY
AND WAS NEVER
SEEN AGAIN**
*MRS. EVANS PILOTED
THE VESSEL SAFELY
TO ITS PIER*

CHANDRAGUPTA MAURYA
ruler of India from 321 B.C. to 297 B.C.
BARRED BY LAW FROM
RESIGNING HIS THRONE
*KILLED HIMSELF BY REFUSING
TO EAT OR DRINK FOR
A PERIOD OF 3 WEEKS*

THE REV. N.P. HACKE
1800-1878
AT THE AGE OF 19
BECAME THE PASTOR OF
CONGREGATIONS IN 4
DIFFERENT COMMUNITIES
IN PENNSYLVANIA
*-AND SERVED ALL OF
THEM CONTINUOUSLY
FOR 59 YEARS*

BUSES in Nigeria,
ALWAYS A HAZARD TO LIFE AND
LIMB, DISPLAY SUCH SIGNS AS
"LOVE YOUR NEIGHBOUR"

HISTORY II - B
SPANISH - A
BIOLOGY - C
HISTORY I - A

THE GRADES OF E.J. **BACA** OF Socorro, N.M., AT THE UNIVERSITY OF NEW MEXICO, ON HIS SOPHOMORE GRADE REPORT *SPELLED OUT HIS LAST NAME*

MR. AND MRS. **PETER PETERSON** of Fairview, Utah, *CELEBRATED THEIR 81ST WEDDING ANNIVERSARY*

IRON SHOES WERE PUT ON THE DEAD in Luristan, Persia, *SO THEY WOULD REMAIN WELL SHOD THROUGHOUT ETERNITY*

EMPEROR JOHN TZIMISCES (925-976) OF THE Byzantine Empire

WHILE GALLOPING PAST ON A FAST HORSE COULD BAT A LEATHER BALL OUT OF A DEEP GLASS BOWL

- HITTING IT HIGH INTO THE AIR -

WITHOUT TOUCHING THE BOWL WITH HIS STICK

THE TOMB THAT CRADLED A COUNTRY'S INDEPENDENCE!

THE MAUSOLEUM of Sher-i-Surkh in Nadirabad WAS THE MEETING PLACE IN 1747 IN WHICH AHMAD SHAH DURRANI WAS CROWNED THE FIRST KING OF AFGHANISTAN *AND THE COUNTRY DECLARED ITS INDEPENDENCE FROM IRAN*

THOMAS HUTCHINSON
of Easingwold, England, A MOUNTED MESSENGER, RODE FROM EASINGWOLD TO YORK AND BACK 5 TIMES IN A SINGLE DAY —A DISTANCE OF 130 MILES

THE CHURCH OF LE PLANÈS
in France
ORIGINALLY WAS CONSTRUCTED AS THE TOMB OF AN ARAB REBEL NAMED MUNAZA WHO WAS EXECUTED DURING A MOORISH INVASION OF FRANCE IN 721

A MARBLE LEDGER in Shogahara Cemetery, in Kobe, Japan, IS THE TOMBSTONE OF THE BRAGA FAMILY, DESCENDANTS OF VINCENTE E. BRAGA, A PORTUGUESE ACCOUNTANT, *WHO INTRODUCED DOUBLE-ENTRY BOOKKEEPING TO JAPAN*

IN LOVING MEMORY OF

139

EVERY PORCH PILLAR OF THE BROADWELL HOUSE IN Cincinnati, Ohio, *WAS THE ENTIRE TRUNK OF A TREE*

Married Women In Garhwal, Himalaya, WEAR UMBRELLA HATS OF LEAVES DURING THE VIOLENT MONSOON RAINS —*BUT TO MAKE SINGLE GIRLS LESS CHOOSY THEY ARE FORBIDDEN TO COVER THEIR HEADS*

THE **Column** OF **AILESBURY,** England, WAS ERECTED IN 1789 *TO MARK THE RECOVERY OF KING GEORGE III FROM A PERIOD OF INSANITY*

THE **"TYNE"** A LIFEBOAT LAUNCHED IN 1833 IS PRESERVED IN South Shields, England, AS A MEMORIAL TO ITS FEAT OF HAVING *RESCUED MORE THAN 1,000 PERSONS*

DR. OLIVER EVERETT (1811-1888) of Dixon, Ill., IN DELIVERING 5,000 BABIES DURING A PERIOD OF 52 YEARS *TRAVELED BY HORSEBACK THE EQUIVALENT OF 18 YEARS*

A COVERED STAIRWAY on Graciosa, in the Azores, DESCENDS 250 FEET IN THE FISSURE OF A MOUNTAIN TO A STRANGE CAVERN LAKE *THAT HAS AN EBB AND TIDE LIKE THE OCEAN*

A CAMEL CAN SURVIVE **A 13% DEHYDRATION** *3% IS FATAL TO MAN*

THE **CHURCH** of GHEMBI MARIAM on Lake Tana, Ethiopia, WAS CONSTRUCTED WITH MORTAR MADE BY GRINDING TOGETHER ANIMAL HIDES AND EGGS

141

MRS. MICHAEL LOWE of Smoky Creek, Tenn., SAVED HERSELF FROM A PURSUING BEAR **BY DISCARDING HER CLOTHING—** *THE BEAR PAUSED MOMENTARILY AT EACH ARTICLE OF CLOTHING, AND MRS. LOWE REACHED THE SAFETY OF HER HOME* (1776)

THE **INSIGNIA** of the King of Nepal IS THE STAR OF DAVID PLUS A SWORD

AHMED of Istanbul, Turkey, *ACTUALLY SWALLOWS LIVE SNAKES*

A **MONUMENT** in Africa
MARKING THE GRAVE OF 2 BROTHERS WHO ESTABLISHED THE BOUNDARY BETWEEN CYRENE AND LIBYA **BY RUNNING TOWARD EACH OTHER FROM THE FARTHEST BORDERS OF THE 2 PROVINCES—** *THE BORDER WAS ESTABLISHED WHERE THEY MET, BUT WHEN ONE BROTHER WAS ACCUSED OF HAVING LOITERED, BOTH INSISTED UPON BEING BURIED ALIVE ON THE BOUNDARY LINE THEY HAD ESTABLISHED*

BLUEBERRIES GROWING IN THE BLACK FOREST, near Bad Teinach, Germany, **ARE SNOW WHITE**

A **BABY** FOUND BESIDE HIS DEAD MOTHER AFTER A SHIPWRECK IN 1684 WAS ADOPTED BY THE REV. HENOCK SINCLAIR of Owthorne, England, WHO NAMED THE CHILD ADAM ALVIN AND RAISED HIM WITH HIS OWN CHILDREN

24 YEARS LATER ADAM WAS HANGED FOR MURDER HAVING BEEN CONVICTED OF KILLING HIS BENEFACTOR AND BURYING HIS BODY IN THE VICARAGE GARDEN

A **WEAPON** USED IN 14TH-CENTURY EUROPE *SERVED AS BOTH A HATCHET AND GUN*

DR. ABNER **HERSEY** of Barnstable, Mass., IN SUMMER AS WELL AS WINTER **ALWAYS SLEPT UNDER 12 WOOL BLANKETS**

A **Temple** near Aburatsubo, Japan, COMPLETE WITH ALTAR AND STATUE, *BUILT BY FISHERMEN TO THEIR GODDESS, BENTEN, INSIDE A SMALL CAVE*

Mary J. **NOURSE** (1817-1908) of Washington, D.C., WAS NEVER SICK, NEVER WORE EYEGLASSES, AND HAD A FINE, LEGIBLE HANDWRITING UNTIL THE DAY OF HER DEATH *- AT THE AGE OF 91*

JUDGE ROBERT WILLIAMSON AFTER WHOM WILLIAMSON COUNTY, Texas, WAS NAMED SUFFERED A MYSTERIOUS FEVER THAT SO BENT HIS RIGHT LEG *HE WORE A PEG LEG ATTACHED TO HIS RIGHT KNEE*

The **BALANCING TRIANGLE** *NATURAL STONE FORMATION* Sahara Desert

THE REV. JOHN BUZZELL (1767-1863) WAS A PREACHER IN North Pearsonfield, Me., **FOR 80 YEARS**

THE MOST PERILOUS PASSAGE IN THE WORLD! HUNZA a state in Himalayan Pakistan CAN BE REACHED ONLY BY A PATH CREATED IN THE SHEER FACE OF AN 18,000-FOOT PEAK *BY PILING LOOSE STONES IN SMALL HOLES CARVED IN THE CLIFF*

THE HORSE RIDDEN BY KING GUSTAVUS ADOLPHUS of Sweden WHEN HE WAS SLAIN IN THE BATTLE OF LUETZEN IN 1632 *HAS BEEN STUFFED AND PRESERVED IN A STOCKHOLM MUSEUM*

5 ONIONS GROWING AS ONE

A DRAWING OF THE SHIP "SEESTERN" DROPPED INTO THE ATLANTIC IN A BOTTLE NORTH OF THE EQUATOR ON CHRISTMAS DAY, 1882, BY A SEAMAN NAMED SACHAU, WAS SEEN AGAIN BY ITS ARTIST *DECORATING A NATIVE HUT ON THE ISLAND OF BARBADOS 20 YEARS LATER*

PRIVATE GRANARIES in the Jamuna Valley, India, ARE LINKED TO THE HOMES OF THEIR OWNERS BY LONG CHAINS ON WHICH ARE STRUNG BELLS —TO SERVE AS BURGLAR ALARMS

THE TREE-HOPPER A FANTASTIC TROPICAL INSECT *THAT RESEMBLES A PREHISTORIC MONSTER*

The **WOMEN WHO SEW UP THEIR OWN FACES!**

FEMALES in the Chukchi Tribe, Asia, TATTOO THEM-SELVES BY *STITCHING DESIGNS ON THEIR FACES WITH A NEEDLE AND DYED THREAD*

Mrs. **GEORGE C. ARATA** of Atherton, Calif., HER GRANDSON, MARK PARMELEE, AND HER GRANDDAUGHTER, LORALYN PARMELEE, *ALL WERE BORN ON JUNE 20TH*

The Vanishing Lake of Andalo, Italy, A **LAKE** 3,600 FEET LONG, 650 FEET WIDE, AND 45 FEET DEEP **THAT DRAINS DRY EACH JUNE**— *THE LAKE BOTTOM YIELDS A HAY HARVEST EACH AUTUMN*— **AFTER WHICH THE LAKE ALWAYS REAPPEARS**

A **RANCH HOUSE**
BUILT IN NEW ENGLAND IN 1849
FOR MARTIN MURPHY, JR.,
*THEN SHIPPED IN SECTIONS
AND REASSEMBLED
IN SUNNYVALE, CALIF.*

THE **FRIENDSHIP COIN**
A THALER WAS MINTED BY
THE DUKE of ZWEIBRUCKEN,
Germany, IN 1754,

EXCLUSIVELY FOR USE AS
*SOUVENIR GIFTS TO
NEIGHBORING PRINCES*

DEMETER DIAMANTIDI
of Vienna
CLIMBED 4 MOUNTAINS
The Schneeberg (6,800 feet)
The Rax (6,600 feet)
The Veitsch (6,200 feet)
The Schneealpe (6,250 feet)
AND DROVE A TOTAL OF 60 MILES
BY CARRIAGE FROM MOUNTAIN TO
MOUNTAIN - *ALL IN 24 HOURS !*

THE **DEAD**
in New Britain,
in the Pacific,
ARE BURIED
UPRIGHT—

IN
BAMBOO
COFFINS

147

2 CHURCHES in Gran, Norway, WERE BUILT SIDE BY SIDE BY 2 FEUDING SISTERS *-EACH OF WHOM HAD VOWED THEY WOULD NEVER BE UNDER THE SAME ROOF*

THE **CATS THAT SWIM** The Sundarbans, India *THEY CATCH FISH WITH THEIR PAWS*

HENRY SOUTHARD of Baskingridge, N.J., WAS A MEMBER OF THE HOUSE OF REPRESENTATIVES FROM NEW JERSEY –

– AND HIS SON, **SAMUEL L. SOUTHARD**

SERVED SIMULTANEOUSLY AS A U.S. SENATOR FROM THE SAME STATE

FATHER AND SON SERVED TOGETHER ON A JOINT CONGRESSIONAL COMMITTEE ON THE MISSOURI COMPROMISE

EVERY DOOR at the Oasis of Hon, in Libya, IS MADE FROM THE TRUNKS OF SACRED DATE PALMS *-IN THE BELIEF THEY WILL SAFEGUARD OCCUPANTS AGAINST ANY INTRUSION*

THE HORSETAIL A PLANT WHICH NOW GROWS TO A HEIGHT OF 6 FEET *IS DESCENDED FROM ONE WHICH IN PREHISTORIC DAYS WAS 100-FEET TALL*

A GRAVE in Pridvorica, Yugoslavia, 40 DAYS AFTER ITS OCCUPANT'S DEATH IS ADORNED WITH WOODEN CROSSES —ONE FOR EACH CLOSE RELATIVE

THE HOUSE BUILT OF LEFTOVERS, Brühl, Germany IT WAS CONSTRUCTED IN 1730 BY THE ARCHITECT OF THE CASTLE OF AUGUSTUSBURG —UTILIZING ONLY THE RUBBLE LEFT FROM ERECTING THE CASTLE

THE LADY POSTMAN of Curral das Freiras, Madeira, MUST DAILY CROSS A 6,000-FOOT MOUNTAIN —WHICH MEANS SHE MUST CLIMB AND DESCEND 24,000 FEET EACH DAY FOR A DAILY WAGE OF 21 CENTS

A HOUSE in Kinver, England, CARVED OUT OF A SINGLE BOULDER

THE MAN WHO REFUSED TO DIE!

HUGH GLASS A GUIDE IN THE BLACK HILLS OF SOUTH DAKOTA WAS SO BADLY CLAWED BY A GRIZZLY BEAR *THAT HIS COMPANIONS LEFT HIM FOR DEAD-* GLASS, WITH A BROKEN LEG AND NO WEAPONS, REACHED FORT KIOWA SEVERAL WEEKS LATER -HAVING CRAWLED 100 MILES ON HIS HANDS AND KNEES!

AN OLD WINDMILL in Stockholm, Sweden, CONVERTED TO USE AS A COFFEEHOUSE

A **LEAD CHEST** CONTAINING 9,000 SILVER PENNIES BURIED BY BISHOP WALKELYN of Winchester, England, IN 1098, WAS FOUND ACCIDENTALLY BY 4 SMALL BOYS AFTER.IT HAD BEEN *FORGOTTEN FOR 735 YEARS*

WEST BOW HOUSE in Edinburgh, Scotland, HAS APPEARED TO BE COLLAPSING FOR 400 YEARS- ITS UPPER STORY PROJECTS 7 FEET, AND THE HOUSE SEEMS TO BE OFF BALANCE

THE REV. PREACHER
THE REV. TEACHER
THE REV. DOCTOR
THE REV. PROCTOR
THE REV. MILLER
THE REV. DISTILLER

A LETTER SO ADDRESSED WAS DELIVERED TO THE REV. JACOB GREEN of Whippany, N.J. -WHO HELD ALL THOSE OCCUPATIONS SIMULTANEOUSLY (1745)

JOSEPH L. D'AURELIO of No. Canton, Ohio, HAS ALL HIS INTERNAL ORGANS -HEART, STOMACH, APPENDIX, ETC.- *ON THE WRONG SIDE OF HIS BODY*

Mrs. **LUELLA SMITH MOTT** of Acton, Mass., AT THE TIME OF HER DEATH IN 1945 AT 76 WAS THE ONLY AMERICAN WHOSE GRANDFATHER HAD FOUGHT IN THE BATTLE OF CONCORD -THE FIRST ENGAGEMENT OF THE AMERICAN REVOLUTION- **170 YEARS EARLIER**

The **ORDER** OF THE **QUEEN OF SHEBA** IS A VERY HIGH DECORATION BESTOWED BY THE EMPEROR OF ETHIOPIA

The **MICHIGAN** FIRST IRON VESSEL OF THE U.S. NAVY, WAS LAUNCHED IN 1844 AND IN ACTIVE SERVICE ON THE GREAT LAKES FOR **75 YEARS**

151

LAUGHING BOY

NATURAL STONE FORMATION

at the mouth of the Restigouche River, New Brunswick Canada

THE **ROOFTOP THAT IS A WATER DIVIDE**
RAIN FALLING ON THE PEAKED ROOF OF A SHED ON THE SCHOLIS FARM, near Lucelle, France,
FLOWS INTO THE MEDITERRANEAN FROM ONE SIDE OF THE ROOF AND FROM THE OTHER SIDE INTO THE NORTH SEA

THE ALTAR TOMB
IN THE CHURCHYARD OF Bournemouth, England,
HAS NEVER HELD A BODY—
IT WAS USED BY SMUGGLERS AS A PLACE OF CONCEALMENT FOR THEIR CONTRABAND

A **PYGMY** OF THE CONGO EXPRESSES SORROW *BY STANDING ON HIS HEAD*

THE **CASTLE of MORIMONT** in Alsace, France, WAS BUILT BY PIERRE DE MORIMONT AS A REPLICA OF A TURKISH PRISON *IN WHICH FOR YEARS HE HAD BEEN INCARCERATED*

KING STANISLAW LESZCZYNSKI (1677-1766) of Poland ATE ONLY ONE MEAL A DAY **FOR 30 YEARS**

THE **MOUNTAIN PEAK THAT WAS GIVEN AS A SOUVENIR AT A DINNER PARTY** **MOUNT USHBA** in the Caucasus, **15,500** FEET HIGH, WAS CLIMBED BY CENCI VON FICKER of Vienna, Austria, IN 1903, AND AT A DINNER TENDERED HER BY PRINCE MAZERI **SHE WAS GIVEN OWNERSHIP OF THE MOUNTAIN**

FAMILY SEALS IN THE GERMANY OF 1800 WERE AVAILABLE WITH A BUST OF EMPEROR FRANCIS II AS THE HANDLE -FOR AN EXTRA TAX OF $10 A YEAR

153

The
CHURCH of SANTA CHIARA
built in Enna, Sicily, in 1563,
BECAME A WAR MEMORIAL IN
1957 AFTER IT HAD BEEN AN
ABANDONED STRUCTURE
FOR 200 YEARS

THE LUCKIEST SMUGGLER IN THE WORLD!

ISAAC GULLIVER (1745-1822)
of Bournemouth, England,
LEADER OF A BAND OF 50 SMUGGLERS,
BECAUSE HE WARNED ENGLAND'S
KING GEORGE III OF A FRENCH PLOT
WAS GIVEN ROYAL PERMISSION
*"TO SMUGGLE AS MUCH
AS HE LIKES"*

PADLOCK
KEYS
USED BY
THE TUAREGS OF THE
Central Sahara Desert,
10 INCHES LONG AND
ELABORATELY CARVED,
*HAVE BEEN MADE THE SAME
WAY FOR 2,000 YEARS*

BLONDIN
THE FAMOUS
ROPE WALKER
CROSSED NIAGARA
FALLS ON A ROPE
*PUSHING AHEAD OF
HIM A LION IN A
WHEELBARROW*

CHRISTIAN PIVETT (1703-1796)
A SCULPTOR of York, England,
BECAUSE HIS HOUSE CAUGHT
FIRE WHILE HE WAS ASLEEP
*NEVER AGAIN SLEPT IN A
BED FOR THE FINAL 32
YEARS OF HIS LIFE*

THE ABBEY OF SAINT-JEAN-des-VIGNES
Soissons, France,
ONE OF THE MOST MAGNIFICENT GOTHIC EDIFICES IN THE WORLD
**IS ONLY A FAÇADE
WITH NO BUILDING BEHIND IT!**
*MOST OF THE STRUCTURE WAS DEMOLISHED IN 1804
BUT ITS FRONT HAS BEEN PRESERVED FOR 158 YEARS*

NEEDLES FOUND IN
A GRAVEYARD
near, Engen,
Germany,
*WERE MADE
OF CHICKEN
BONES
2,000
YEARS AGO.*

A **BOTTLE**
CONTAINING A NOTE
DESCRIBING THE FATAL INJURY
OF CHUNOSUKE MATSUYAMA AND THE DEATH
OF 44 SHIPMATES ON A HUNT FOR BURIED TREASURE IN 1784 WAS
WASHED ASHORE AT MATSUYAMA'S OWN VILLAGE IN JAPAN 151 YEARS LATER

King
HENRI III
of France
ATE A TURKEY DINNER IN 1575
—45 YEARS BEFORE THE PILGRIMS LANDED IN THE NEW WORLD

THE CHIMES
Red Canon, So. Dakota,
A CLUSTER OF STALACTITES
WHICH PRODUCE BEAUTIFUL
MELODIES WHEN TAPPED
IN PROPER SEQUENCE

Hans
SOMMERMATTER
1430 - 1556
of St. Niklaus, Switzerland,
MARRIED A WOMAN OF 30
AS HIS SECOND WIFE
WHEN HE WAS
100 YEARS OF AGE
*AND BECAME A FATHER
THE FOLLOWING YEAR*
HE LIVED TO BE **126**

THE MAN WHO REHEARSED HIS OWN FUNERAL!

Emperor Charles V of Germany

3 WEEKS BEFORE HIS DEATH WRAPPED HIMSELF IN HIS SHROUD, WAS PLACED IN HIS COFFIN AND JOINED IN THE REQUIEM HYMNS—

WITH SERVANTS CARRYING BLACK CANDLES IN HIS FUNERAL PROCESSION

September, 1558

John MILDENHALL

A MILLER of Cricklade, England,

COULD SIGN HIS NAME ON THE CEILING

WHILE A 56-POUND WEIGHT HUNG BY A STRING FROM HIS THUMB

THE BIT OF ROMAN EMPEROR CONSTANTINE THE GREAT'S HORSE

IS STILL PRESERVED IN THE CHURCH OF ST. SIFFREIN, Carpentras, France

THE **CAMOUFLE TOWER** in Metz, France, WAS CONSTRUCTED IN 1437 BY JACQUES DE CAMOUFLE, AN ARMY CANNONEER, AT HIS OWN EXPENSE - *IN EXCHANGE FOR PERMISSION TO FIRE A CANNON ATOP IT* **3 TIMES A DAY IN ANY DIRECTION HE PLEASED**

THE **TIMEPIECE** IN THE **CITY HALL** of Bergamo, Italy, IS A UNIQUE SUNDIAL MARKED OUT **ON THE FLOOR BENEATH A PORCH** *THE INDICATOR WHICH CASTS THE TIME-TELLING SHADOW HANGS FROM THE TOP OF AN ARCHWAY*

POST CARD MAILED FROM Princeton, N.J., AND DELIVERED TO CHARLES A. KEARNS OF Wayne, N.J.

ALTHOUGH IT CARRIED NO NAME OR ADDRESS

Catherine **SEDGWICK** (1789-1867) NOTED NOVELIST of Stockbridge, Mass., NEVER MARRIED ALTHOUGH SHE WAS WOOED BY **48 SUCCESSIVE SUITORS**

THE **NEEDLE'S EYE** *NATURAL ROCK FORMATION* So. Dakota

158

MRS. NAO DEGUCHI (1836-1918)
of Ayabe, Japan,
AFTER FALLING INTO A TRANCE
IN 1892 WROTE A VOLUME
OF 200,000 PAGES
*—WHICH AFTER HER DEATH
BECAME THE HOLY BOOK OF
A NEW SECT CALLED "OOMOTO"*

THE MOCK RUINS,
in Virginia Water, England,
WERE BUILT BY KING GEORGE III
JUST TO MAKE USE OF SOME
ANCIENT STONES HE HAD
FOUND IN THE COURTYARD
OF THE BRITISH MUSEUM

James Fenimore COOPER
BECAME A NOVELIST
ONLY BECAUSE HIS WIFE ONCE
ASKED HIM TO READ TO HER—
*THE NOVEL HE READ ALOUD WAS
JANE AUSTEN'S "PRIDE AND
PREJUDICE," WHICH COOPER
FINALLY TOSSED ASIDE IN
DISGUST AND SAID:"I COULD
WRITE A BETTER NOVEL MYSELF"*

159

BROADHURST
AN ESTATE IN ENGLAND,
WAS LEASED FROM
1276 TO 1535
FOR A RENTAL OF ONE POUND
OF PEPPER A YEAR

THE PEOPLE WHO CAN WALK BAREFOOTED AMONG VENOMOUS SNAKES!

MUKUBAL TRIBESMEN
in Angola, Portuguése Africa, NEVER WEAR SHOES
—YET THE AREA IS INFESTED WITH POISONOUS SNAKES

EACH MAN, WOMAN AND CHILD WEARS A LEATHER BAG FILLED WITH A SECRET SNAKE BITE ANTIDOTE WHICH IS APPLIED DIRECTLY TO THE WOUND
—AND NO ONE IN THE TRIBE HAS EVER DIED OF A SNAKE BITE

Stone IN WHICH WATER HAS WASHED OUT A PERFECT SQUARE

BUFFALO SKULLS
WERE PAINTED BY THE PLAINS INDIANS AND LEFT ON THE PRAIRIES WITH GIFTS SO THE GREAT SPIRIT WOULD SEND THE INDIANS *A REINCARNATION OF EACH BUFFALO THEY HAD KILLED*

THE OLD MAN
NATURAL STONE FORMATION
Red Canon, South Dakota

160

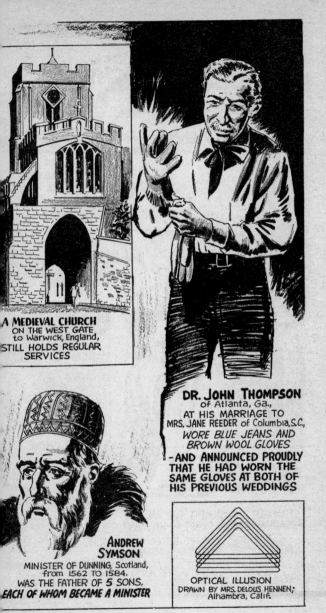

A MEDIEVAL CHURCH
ON THE WEST GATE
to Warwick, England,
STILL HOLDS REGULAR
SERVICES

DR. JOHN THOMPSON
of Atlanta, Ga.,
AT HIS MARRIAGE TO
MRS. JANE REEDER of Columbia, S.C.,
WORE BLUE JEANS AND
BROWN WOOL GLOVES
—AND ANNOUNCED PROUDLY
THAT HE HAD WORN THE
SAME GLOVES AT BOTH OF
HIS PREVIOUS WEDDINGS

ANDREW
SYMSON
MINISTER OF DUNNING, Scotland,
from 1562 TO 1584,
WAS THE FATHER OF 5 SONS,
EACH OF WHOM BECAME A MINISTER

OPTICAL ILLUSION
DRAWN BY MRS. DELOUS HENNEN,
Alhambra, Calif.

THE STRANGEST COMMUNITY IN THE WORLD

SHAHR A TOWN IN the desert of Lut, Persia, WAS CREATED BY NATURE ITS MANY-STORIED STRUCTURES RESEMBLING CASTLES HAVING BEEN *CARVED OUT BY THE WIND* NOMADS LATER DUG OUT CHAMBERS AND THUS CONVERTING THE ILLUSION INTO A REAL TOWN

A DOOR in Winchester, England, WHICH KING CHARLES II USED TO VISIT NELL GWYNNE *WAS SEALED SO NO OTHER SWEETHEARTS COULD EVER AGAIN USE IT*

THE STRANGEST "PUNISHMENT" FOR AN ASSASSINATION ATTEMPT IN HISTORY!

NICEPHORUS COURT JESTER TO BYZANTINE EMPEROR CONSTANTINE X, APPREHENDED IN AN ATTEMPT TO PLUNGE A DAGGER INTO THE MONARCH WAS DRESSED IN THE EMPEROR'S PURPLE HABIT AND CROWN AND SEATED ON HIS THRONE—BECAUSE CONSTANTINE FELT THIS WOULD *SATISFY THE JESTER'S CRAVING TO REPLACE HIS MASTER*

James RICHARDSON of Askrigg, England WORE THE SAME HAT AND BOOTS FOR **42 YEARS**

SHINING BOTH HIS HAT AND FOOTGEAR WITH THE SAME POLISH AND CLOTH EVERY DAY

A **MONUMENT** ERECTED ON THE BANKS of Loch Shiel, Scotland, IN MEMORY OF BONNIE PRINCE CHARLIE *BECAME ALSO A MEMORIAL TO ITS BUILDER, ALEXANDER MACDONALD, WHEN HE DIED SUDDENLY DURING ITS CONSTRUCTION AT THE AGE OF 28*

BONE SHAPED LIKE **A SKULL**

ZITHERS ARE MADE BY THE NATIVES of Pahang, Malaya, OUT OF GREEN BAMBOO —WITH STRIPS OF BARK FORMING THE STRINGS

163

MRS. OLGA HOPGOOD
of South Caulfield, Australia,
AFTER BEING TOTALLY BLIND FOR 15 YEARS
AND VIRTUALLY SIGHTLESS FOR 40 YEARS
*SUDDENLY REGAINED HER VISION
AT THE AGE OF 77*

YARMOUTH
A TOWN ON THE
Isle of Wight, England,
SENT 2 REPRESENTATIVES
TO PARLIAMENT
FOR 300 YEARS
*-YET IT NEVER HAD MORE
THAN 9 VOTERS*

A **GRAVE** in Java,
WITH AN UMBRELLA TO SHIELD
THE DECEASED FROM THE SUN,
AND HIS FAVORITE BOWL CRACKED
*TO SYMBOLIZE THE PASSING OF
HIS SOUL INTO THE BEYOND*

**CHERRY TREE
BRANCH**
MARKED BY
NATURE
*WITH THE
LETTER "C"*

THE
TENREC
of Madagascar, *ONLY 16" IN LENGTH,*
LIVES ON EARTHWORMS 3 FEET LONG

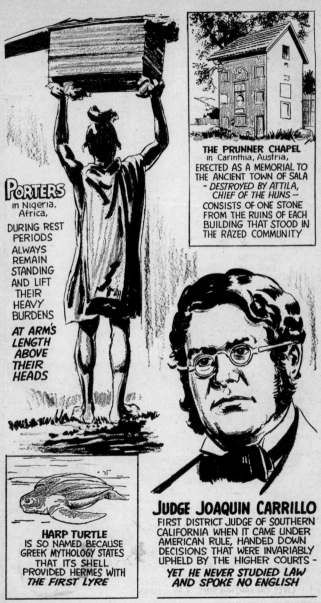

PORTERS
in Nigeria, Africa,
DURING REST PERIODS ALWAYS REMAIN STANDING AND LIFT THEIR HEAVY BURDENS *AT ARM'S LENGTH ABOVE THEIR HEADS*

THE PRUNNER CHAPEL
in Carinthia, Austria,
ERECTED AS A MEMORIAL TO THE ANCIENT TOWN OF SALA — *DESTROYED BY ATTILA, CHIEF OF THE HUNS* — CONSISTS OF ONE STONE FROM THE RUINS OF EACH BUILDING THAT STOOD IN THE RAZED COMMUNITY

HARP TURTLE
IS SO NAMED BECAUSE GREEK MYTHOLOGY STATES THAT ITS SHELL PROVIDED HERMES WITH *THE FIRST LYRE*

JUDGE JOAQUIN CARRILLO
FIRST DISTRICT JUDGE OF SOUTHERN CALIFORNIA WHEN IT CAME UNDER AMERICAN RULE, HANDED DOWN DECISIONS THAT WERE INVARIABLY UPHELD BY THE HIGHER COURTS — *YET HE NEVER STUDIED LAW AND SPOKE NO ENGLISH*

165

PROLOGUE CAMPOS of Pará, Brazil, HAS 3 BROTHERS NAMED **CHAPTER, ERRORS,** and **EPILOGUE**

TABLE ROCK NATURAL FORMATION THAT STOOD FOR YEARS IN LINCOLN COUNTY, KANSAS

The Rev. **Thomas LINDLEY** WAS CURATE OF HALTON GILL, England, **FOR 70 YEARS**

"TIGER" A DOG OWNED BY CHRISTINE ALBERT, SHELLS AND EATS INDIAN NUTS Maspeth, N.Y.

THE **Temple OF TARISI** Tibet IS ROOFED WITH SOLID-GOLD TILES VALUED TODAY AT **$173,250!**

WINE DELIVERIES
TO ANCIENT BABYLON WERE
MADE VIA THE EUPHRATES RIVER
*IN ROUND BOATS THAT ALWAYS
CARRIED A DONKEY* –

AT BABYLON THE BOATS WERE
SOLD BECAUSE THEY COULD NOT
BE PROPELLED UPRIVER
AGAINST THE CURRENT – AND
THE TRIP HOME WAS MADE
ON THE DONKEY

WOOD MARKED WITH
A PERFECT STAR

FARMERS in the
Valley
of Biros,
France,
STILL
WEAR SHOES
WITH HIGH,
TURNED-UP
TOES –

*A STYLE
INTRODUCED
BY KING
RICHARD II*
of England
*AT HIS
WEDDING
TO ISABELLA,
DAUGHTER
OF KING
CHARLES VI*
of France
IN 1396

A HUGE PALACE
WAS BUILT ANNUALLY in Montreal, Canada,
FOR 10 SUCCESSIVE YEARS FROM 1883
TO 1892 *FROM BLOCKS OF ICE*

167

MR. **COPP** IS PUBLISHER OF A
MAGAZINE FOR **POLICEMEN**
New York City

THE **TOWER** OF THE ANCIENT
MONASTERY OF **WESSOBRUNN**,
in Bavaria, Germany,
*HAS A SUNDIAL FOR USE IN THE
DAYTIME AND A CLOCK FOR
TELLING TIME AT NIGHT*

**AHMED
BEDESSI**
BEARING NEWS OF THE ASSASSINATION OF A LOCAL CHIEFTAIN,
RODE FROM Sistan, Afghanistan, TO Kerman, Persia—340 MILES IN 3 DAYS—
AND MADE THE ENTIRE JOURNEY ON THE SAME CAMEL

PAYMENT
OF BLACKMAIL
BY A SPECIAL
LAW PASSED IN
1567
IN SCOTLAND
*WAS PUNISHABLE
BY DEATH!*

THE **MANOR**
OF
MONGEWELL
in England

FOR SEVERAL
CENTURIES
UNTIL 1930
*CONSTITUTED
A COMPLETE
PARISH*

168

MR. **BREWER** of Brentford, England, LIVES ON **DISTILLERY ROAD**

THE **STONE CHURCH of SCHARZFELD** Germany BUILT INSIDE AN ANCIENT CAVE FOR THE FIRST CHRISTIAN SERVICES HELD IN THE AREA, HAS AN ALTAR, PULPIT AND PEWS *CARVED OUT OF SOLID ROCK*

ROBERT MORRIS (1734-1806) A SIGNER OF THE DECLARATION OF INDEPENDENCE *ACTUALLY VOTED AGAINST THE DECLARATION IN CONGRESS!*

AN **AMPHITHEATRE** ON THE CAMPUS of Bradfield College, England - AN EXACT REPRODUCTION OF THE AMPHITHEATRE OF EPIDAURUS IN ANCIENT GREECE - WAS CREATED BY *CARVING IT ENTIRELY FROM CHALK*

HERMAN MARCUS of Vicksburg, Miss., PLAYING GOLF AT THE VICKSBURG COUNTRY CLUB IN 1937, SHOT A HOLE-IN-ONE ON THE SECOND HOLE - *AND SCORED ANOTHER HOLE-IN-ONE 25 YEARS LATER ON THE SAME HOLE*

169

4-LEGGED CHICKEN

John **PARRY**
famed 18th-century harpist,
WAS THE BEST CHECKERS
PLAYER IN ALL WALES
-YET HE WAS TOTALLY BLIND

THE **MISTAKE THAT SAVED A CITY!**
THE MANGIA TOWER, in Siena, Italy,
WAS NAMED FOR ITS FIRST
BELLRINGER, WHO RANG THE
BELLS BY ERROR IN 1348
-AROUSING THE TOWNSPEOPLE
JUST IN TIME TO FIGHT OFF
A MIDNIGHT ATTACK

AN AUTOMOBILE
in the Technical Museum
of Vienna, Austria,
INVENTED BY
SIEGFRIED MARCUS IN 1875
IS CLAIMED TO BE THE
FIRST GASOLINE-DRIVEN
CAR IN HISTORY

A **TOMBSTONE**
IN THE
CHURCHYARD
of Thursley, England,
ERECTED IN 1786 OVER
THE GRAVE OF AN
ANONYMOUS SAILOR,
IDENTIFIES HIM BY
AN ILLUSTRATION
OF HIS MURDER
BY 3 FOOTPADS

170

THE **BIRCH LEAF ROLLER** PROVIDES A CONTAINER FOR ITS EGGS AND FOOD FOR THE EMERGING LARVA BY MAKING EXACT INCISIONS IN A BIRCH LEAF *AND THEN ROLLING IT TO FORM AN INGENIOUS CONE*

THE MALBONE MANSION in Newport, R.I., BURNED TO THE GROUND BECAUSE THE HAUGHTY MRS. MALBONE *REFUSED TO PERMIT THE RURAL FIRE FIGHTERS TO TRAMP THROUGH HER HOME*

A **MARRIED WOMAN** of the Sudan WEARS HER GOLD WEDDING RING *IN HER NOSE*

THE **WEATHER VANE** OVER FABULOUS SCOTTY'S CASTLE IN Death Valley, Calif., *DEPICTS SCOTTY FRYING BACON*

A **STRAW BOAT** IS BUILT BY MEDICINE MEN OF THE SEMAI SENOI TRIBE, in Perak, Malaya, *SO THE ILLNESS OF THEIR PATIENTS CAN BE FLOATED AWAY*

TEWKESBURY ABBEY
England
BUILT IN 1123 AND ORDERED DESTROYED BY KING HENRY VIII, WAS SAVED WHEN SCHOOLCHILDREN DONATED $2,101 TO THE ROYAL TREASURY —
AND IT IS STILL IN SERVICE TODAY

Jenny LIND FOR HER CONCERT TOUR OF THE UNITED STATES IN 1850, WAS PAID $175,000

- BUT P.T. BARNUM'S FEE AS HER MANAGER WAS $500,000

George W. FARIS
of Fort Worth, Texas,
MARRIED 3 SISTERS —
HE WAS MARRIED TO THE FIRST FOR 6 YEARS, TO THE SECOND FOR 42 YEARS - AND MARRIED THE THIRD AT THE AGE OF 80

THE JOHN B. PARSONS HOME FOR THE AGED in Salisbury, Mo.,
BUILT WITH A BEQUEST OF $1,000,000 BY PARSONS, WAS DESIGNED DURING HIS LIFETIME AND THE SITE WAS PURCHASED — *BUT HE DELAYED THE ACTUAL CONSTRUCTION SO HE WOULD NOT BE RECOGNIZED AS A PHILANTHROPIST UNTIL AFTER HIS DEATH*

THE STRANGEST SAFE-DEPOSIT VAULTS IN THE WORLD *THE GRAVES OF SAINTS* in Zeramra, Algeria, ARE CONSIDERED SO SAFE FROM DEPREDATION BY THIEVES THAT NATIVES PILE ALL KINDS OF POSSESSIONS OUTSIDE THEM *— EVEN THEIR HIGHLY VALUED FIREWOOD*

Florence JACOBS of West New York, N.J., COULD RECITE THE ALPHABET AT THE AGE OF **11 MONTHS** *AND WAS ISSUED HER OWN PUBLIC LIBRARY CARD WHEN SHE WAS ONLY 2½ YEARS OF AGE*

A **REPLICA** of the **SANTA MARIA - EXACT IN SIZE AND EVERY DETAIL** HAS BEEN ERECTED BENEATH A STATUE OF COLUMBUS ON THE WHARF OF THE GATE OF PEACE IN BARCELONA, SPAIN

CHRISTOPHER COLUMBUS

DISCOVERED AMERICA ON THE VOYAGE THAT

STARTED ON A **FRIDAY** FIRST SIGHTED LAND ON A **FRIDAY** STARTED HOME ON A **FRIDAY** AND REACHED SPAIN ON A **FRIDAY!**

HIS SECOND, THIRD AND FOURTH VOYAGES EACH BEGAN AND ENDED ON A WEDNESDAY - AND HE DIED ON A WEDNESDAY!

THE **FIRE CHIEF** of Sackets Harbor, N.Y., *IS NAMED* **BURNUP**

The **STRANGE SIGNATURE** of Christopher Columbus

.S. .A. .S. X M Y Xpo FERENS

ACTUALLY REPEATS HIS NAME 3 TIMES -

THE DOUBLE DOTS WITH EACH LETTER S REPRESENT COLONS - AND COLON IS SPANISH FOR **COLUMBUS**

BRONZE KNOCKER ON A DOOR IN KINSKY PALACE, Vienna, Austria, - SO ELABORATE IT REQUIRED **10 YEARS TO CREATE** IT

174

THE ESTATE THAT GAVE US THE "DOILY"

The Manor of Fishill (England) WAS GRANTED BY WILLIAM THE CONQUEROR IN 1067 TO ROBERT D'OILY FOR AN ANNUAL RENTAL CONSISTING OF ONE NAPKIN

CENTURIES LATER WOMEN OF THE D'OILY FAMILY DECIDED THE NAPKIN SENT TO THE KING EACH YEAR SHOULD BE EMBROIDERED — *AND THAT WAS THE ORIGIN OF THE WORD "DOILY"*

William TATHAM of Richmond, Va., AN AMERICAN SOLDIER AND ENGINEER, COMMITTED SUICIDE ON WASHINGTON'S BIRTHDAY IN 1819 *BY LEAPING IN FRONT OF A CANNON JUST AS IT WAS FIRED AS A SALUTE TO THE HOLIDAY*

RAVEL CASTLE in France WAS BUILT WITH 365 WINDOWS — ONE FOR EACH DAY OF THE YEAR

NATURE'S SIGNPOST A **HUGE** BOULDER in the Libyan Desert HAS AN OPENING SHAPED LIKE AN ARROW, AND ALTHOUGH SHIFTING SANDS OBSCURE OTHER GUIDEPOSTS THE *ARROW ALWAYS POINTS THE WAY TO THE NEAREST WATER*

THE **NAME** of the **LAST KING OF KAFFA** Africa WAS KNOWN TO ONLY **7 PEOPLE**—

THE SEVEN DIGNITARIES GAVE THE MONARCH THE NAME **GAKI SHEROTSKO** —AND KEPT IT SECRET IN THE BELIEF THE KING **COULD NOT BE HARMED BY ANYONE WHO DIDN'T KNOW HIS NAME**

Benny CROOK of Winnsboro, La., AGE 13, LIVING NORMALLY AND ATTENDING SCHOOL **WITH AN AIR-GUN PELLET IN HIS HEART**

THE **GOLDEN DOMES OF KADIMAIN** Bagdad THE CUPOLAS OF THIS MOSQUE ARE COVERED WITH SHEETS OF **SOLID GOLD ONE INCH THICK** AND VALUED AT $1,300,000!

THE **PORTLAND VASE** PRESERVED IN THE BRITISH MUSEUM WAS THE URN USED TO HOLD THE ASHES OF ROMAN EMPEROR ALEXANDER SEVERUS AND THOSE OF HIS MOTHER *1726 YEARS AGO*

William Gordon STABLES 1840-1910 of Scotland

WROTE 3 BOOKS EACH YEAR FOR A PERIOD OF 40 YEARS

WILLIAM LEDFORD of Spruce Pine, N.C., 102 YEARS OF AGE, AND HIS WIFE, WHO IS 101

CELEBRATED THEIR 81ST WEDDING ANNIVERSARY

A PERFECT FOSSIL OF A FISH CALLED Pterichthys Milleri FOUND IN RED SANDSTONE NEAR Tomintoul, Scotland, *AND ESTIMATED TO BE 300,000,000 YEARS OLD*

THE **ALLIGATOR** A BURMESE 3-STRINGED GUITAR IS BELIEVED BY NATIVES TO HAVE A *PACIFYING INFLUENCE ON ALLIGATORS*

THE QUEEN'S STEPS
A STAIRWAY BYPASSING
THE GATE TO BYWARD TOWER
IN THE TOWER OF LONDON,
England,
*CAN BE USED ONLY BY
THE QUEEN HERSELF*

MANUEL BUTRON
of San Juan Bautista, Calif.,
WAS CURED OF EPILEPSY
– *WHEN HE WAS SHOT
THROUGH THE CHEST BY
A CRAZED GUNMAN*

A **6 LB.
BASS**
HOOKED IN
Coffee Hill Lake,
near Bonham, Texas,
ESCAPED TRAILING A
15-FOOT STRINGER

*BUT WAS CAUGHT
AGAIN BY
HAROLD ANDERS
8 DAYS LATER*

THE **TEMPLE of FONG TU**
ON THE MOUNTAIN OF HEAVEN,
in China,
FOR A CHARGE OF $1 EACH
SELLS PASSPORTS TO HEAVEN

NUNS WHO SERVE AS NURSES IN THE HOSPITAL OF BEAUNE, France, ARE THE ONLY WOMEN IN THE WORLD WHO STILL WEAR THE HIGH CONICAL HEADDRESS INTRODUCED BY FRENCHWOMEN IN *THE 15TH CENTURY*

THE **MONARCH** WHO DIETED OFF 1,280 POUNDS!

KING EDWARD VII of England WENT ON A STRINGENT DIET AT THE GERMAN SPA OF HOMBURG ANNUALLY FOR 32 YEARS -AND LOST 40 POUNDS EACH YEAR

THE **KNAVE** in the Valley of Ghezendi, in the Sahara Desert

A *NATURAL ROCK FORMATION*

179

MESILLA, *A TOWN IN NEW MEXICO* DURING THE PERIOD BETWEEN 1848 AND 1853 CHANGED ITS NATIONAL ALLEGIANCE **AS OFTEN AS 5 TIMES A WEEK!**

THE RIO GRANDE MARKED THE BOUNDARY BETWEEN THE U.S. AND MEXICO- AND IT CHANGED ITS COURSE SO FREQUENTLY **RESIDENTS OF MESILLA PAID TAXES TO BOTH COUNTRIES**

ELIJAH COALMAN

A FAMED MOUNTAIN GUIDE CLIMBED MT. HOOD, IN OREGON, (11,253 FEET HIGH) *586 TIMES IN 31 YEARS* (1897-1928)

THE TOWER of the PARISH CHURCH of Bishopstoke, England, APPEARED SO SHAKY IN 1887 THAT THE ADJACENT CHURCH WAS DEMOLISHED AS A SAFEGUARD TO WORSHIPERS -YET THE TOWER IS STILL STANDING 74 YEARS LATER

THE **STRANGEST** STORAGE LOCKERS IN THE WORLD **CAVES** in Nalut, Libya, CARVED IN THE FAÇADE OF THE 1,000-YEAR-OLD CRUSADERS' CASTLE AND EACH EQUIPPED WITH AN 8-FOOT DOOR AND A STOUT LOCK, *HAVE BEEN USED TO STORE FOOD BY THE SAME FAMILIES FOR CENTURIES*

STEPHEN **PHARAOH** SON OF A KING OF THE MONTAUK INDIANS, WALKED FROM BROOKLYN TO MONTAUK *-A DISTANCE OF 140 MILES- IN A SINGLE DAY*

Henry **BELSCHNER** of Green Bay, Wis., CELEBRATED THE **70**TH ANNIVERSARY *OF HIS 3d MARRIAGE*

THE SPHINX OF THE SAHARA near Garet el-Luban, in the Sahara Desert *NATURAL ROCK FORMATION*

THE
AUSTRALIAN DRAGONFLY
IS THE FASTEST INSECT
IN THE WORLD – IT CAN
FLY 55 MILES PER HOUR

THE QUEEN WHO PREFERRED DEATH TO RESCUE BY A COMMONER!

QUEEN SUNUNDA, WIFE OF
KING RAMA V of Siam, DROWNED WITH
HER 2 CHILDREN IN THE MENAM RIVER
– BECAUSE IT HAD BEEN MADE A
CRIME PUNISHABLE BY DEATH
FOR A COMMONER TO EVEN TOUCH
THE QUEEN OR HER OFFSPRING
(1881)

RAS MIKAEL

Chief of the Wollo-Galla Tribe,
MARRIED THE DAUGHTER OF KING MENELIK of Ethiopia
WHO HAD CAPTURED HIM AND GIVEN THE PRISONER
THE ALTERNATIVE OF MARRIAGE OR DEATH –
THEY LIVED HAPPILY EVER AFTER

MISS **KNEEBONE** MARRIED **MR. FOOTE** Reno, Nev.

SOUTHAMPTON HOUSE
in Chaptico, Md.,
THE OLDEST FRAME HOUSE IN THE STATE, WAS BUILT IN 1640 *WITH LUMBER BROUGHT FROM ENGLAND*

IT HAS NO DOOR KNOBS AND ITS DOORS ARE STILL OPENED **BY PULLING GOLD CHAINS WHICH RELEASE THE LATCHES**

THE WELLINGTON ARCH in London, England, *HAS A POLICE STATION INSIDE ITS WALLS*

JOHN BROWN
1722 - 1787
A SHEEP HERDER OF Haddington, Scotland,
TAUGHT HIMSELF
GREEK, LATIN, HEBREW, ARABIC, SYRIAC, PERSIAN, ETHIOPIAN, FRENCH, SPANISH, DUTCH, GERMAN AND ITALIAN

183

THE **QUETTA** **MEMORIAL CATHEDRAL** on Thursday Island, Australia, COMMEMORATES THE WRECK OF THE LINER "QUETTA" WHICH SANK IN A CALM SEA AND UNDER A BRIGHT MOON WITH *THE LOSS OF 133 LIVES*

KING CHARLES
1246-1309
of Sicily

WAS THE FATHER OF *2 KINGS, 2 QUEENS, AN EMPEROR AND A SAINT*

Charles OVEREND
WAS ORGANIST OF THE Church of Cleckheaton, England, FOR 49 YEARS – *YET HE NEVER ACCEPTED A PENNY IN PAY* AND HAD BEEN BLIND FROM THE AGE OF 9 MONTHS (1822-1871)

THE CHECKERED HAIRY SNAIL (*Trichotropis cancellata*) HAS GRAY AND BROWN HAIR GROWING ON ITS SHELL

John BLACK
of Vincennes, Ind.,

CARRIED A BARREL OF SALT WEIGHING **224** POUNDS FROM THE STORE TO HIS FARM *WALKING 2 MILES WITH THE BARREL IN HIS ARMS!*

MEETING A NEIGHBOR ON THE ROAD HE CHATTED FOR **45** MINUTES – AND NEVER EVEN SHIFTED HIS LOAD TO A MORE COMFORTABLE POSITION

CHRIST CHURCH GATE in Canterbury, England, AN ARCHITECTURAL MASTERPIECE CONSTRUCTED IN 1517 *HAD ITS UPPER BATTLEMENTS REMOVED 300 YEARS LATER SO PASSERSBY COULD MORE EASILY SEE THE CLOCK ON CANTERBURY CATHEDRAL*

A **BABY TAPIR** IS STRIPED – YET THE ADULTS ARE NOT

HUNGRY MOTHER STATE PARK in Virginia GETS ITS NAME FROM THE WORDS A CHILD WAS MURMURING OVER AND OVER TO A MOTHER MURDERED BY INDIANS:

"Hungry, Mother! Hungry, Mother!"

EMPEROR IVAN VI of Russia WHO ASSUMED THE THRONE IN 1740 AT THE AGE OF 2 MONTHS, RULED FOR **404 DAYS - THEN SPENT 23 YEARS IN SOLITARY CONFINEMENT** HE WAS FINALLY MURDERED ON ORDERS FROM CATHERINE THE GREAT

A **HORSE** WAS HOISTED TO THE BELFRY OF St. Mary's Church, Georgia, BY A GANG OF SMUGGLERS TO DIVERT ATTENTION OF THE DOCK GUARDS *WHILE A CARGO OF CONTRABAND WAS BEING UNLOADED*

THE CUPOLA ON HARRY WESTERHOFF'S BARN near Garland, Nebr., *FORMERLY WAS THE DOME OF NEBRASKA'S FIRST STATE CAPITOL*

ROBERT M. DOUGLAS
of Vincennes, Indiana,
WAS DROWNED CROSSING THE WABASH RIVER IN 1807
ON HIS WAY TO THE PREMIERE OF A PLAY ENTITLED
"DROWNING MEN CLUTCH AT STRAWS"

"COCKEYED" CHARLIE
CONSIDERED
ONE OF THE BEST
STAGE DRIVERS IN
OLD CALIFORNIA,
LIVED AND VOTED AS A
MAN FROM 1848 UNTIL 1879
—WHEN DEATH REVEALED
"COCKEYED CHARLIE" ACTUALLY WAS A
GIRL NAMED CHARLOTTE PARKHURST

GUILLAUME BRIÇONNET

(1468-1533) FRENCH AMBASSADOR TO ROME,

UNABLE TO WALK BECAUSE OF THE GOUT,

TRAINED A DONKEY TO CARRY HIM FROM ROOM TO ROOM IN HIS PALACE, *RECEIVED VISITORS AND DINED ON THE DONKEY'S BACK* **AND EVEN SAT ASTRIDE THE DONKEY WHILE WORKING AT HIS DESK**

THE **GRAVES** OF EDWIN AND MARGARET YOUNG ARE CIRCLED BY THE GRAVES OF THEIR 8 CHILDREN *- NOT ONE OF WHOM SURVIVED INFANCY* West Bay Cemetery, Gouldsboro, Me.

THE **POSTAGE CANCELLATION** USED BY THE POSTMASTER of Headtide, Me., IN 1883 WAS IN THE FORM OF THE HEAD OF A CIGAR STORE INDIAN

SIR CHRISTOPHER WREN

1632-1723 WHO BUILT ST. PAUL'S CATHEDRAL, in London, England,

WAS THE FIRST PERSON TO BE INTERRED WITHIN ITS WALLS

THE TALLEST DOGHOUSE IN THE WORLD
Sudbury, Ontario

A 30-FOOT-HIGH DOGHOUSE BUILT BY EMIL FERA AND JOHN CLEMENS FOR THEIR 3 AFGHANS IS COMPLETELY AIR-CONDITIONED, HAS A KITCHEN ON THE FIRST FLOOR AND *BEDS WITH WHITE SHEETS IN THE THIRD-FLOOR BEDROOM SUITE*

A WOMAN of the WATUSI Tribe, in Africa,
DONS A SET OF WHITE BANDS ON THE DAY SHE FIRST BECOMES A MOTHER
AND IT IS FORBIDDEN TO REMOVE THEM FROM HER —EVEN IN DEATH

A CHIMNEY in Istria, Yugoslavia,
THAT IS SHAPED LIKE A CORKSCREW
AND PUFFS OUT SMOKE IN SPIRALS

THE ROCK THAT GROWS Zanzibar
IT INCREASES 1½ INCHES IN LENGTH EACH YEAR

THE **EARL of BELMORE**
1740-1802
WAS PAID $150,000 BY THE
BRITISH GOVERNMENT AS
COMPENSATION FOR THE LOSS OF
THE 2 PARLIAMENTARY SEATS OF
BALLYSHANNON, IRELAND
*- WHICH HIS FAMILY HAD
CONTROLLED FOR 187 YEARS*

QABR HUD A TOWN
in Hadhramaut, Arabia,
IS INHABITED ONLY DURING
THE ANNUAL PILGRIMAGE TO
THE GRAVE OF THE PROPHET HUD
- A TOTAL OF 3 DAYS IN EACH YEAR

THE WATER SUPPLY SYSTEM
in the Canton of Valais, Switzerland,
CONSISTS OF 15,000 MILES
OF WOODEN TROUGHS –
*MADE BY HOLLOWING OUT
THE TRUNKS OF TREES*
THESE PIPES ARE CARRIED ALONG
THE SHEER FACE OF PRECIPICES
BY PEGS DRIVEN INTO THE SOLID ROCK
*- A FEAT THAT ANNUALLY CLAIMS
THE LIVES OF MORE SWISS THAN
DO AVALANCHES AND STORMS*

THE **REV. JOSEPH ADAMS**
1689-1783
WAS A PASTOR IN Newington, N.H.,
FOR 68 YEARS
*HIS GREAT-GREAT-GREAT-GREAT-
GREAT-GRANDDAUGHTER
LIVES IN THE HOUSE BUILT
AS HIS PARSONAGE*

RUBY FALLS
145 FEET HIGH
IS 1,120 FEET BELOW THE SURFACE OF THE EARTH
Lookout Mt. Caves, Tenn.

THE REV. SOL STODDARD
(1643-1729) of Northampton, Mass.,
HAD **5** DAUGHTERS
- AND MARRIED EVERY ONE OF THEM TO A MINISTER

A **PLOW** In Algeria
PULLED BY A CAMEL AND A DONKEY

THE **MORTAR** USED BY the Jakuts of Siberia TO GRIND TOBACCO LEAF INTO SNUFF *IS THE HOLLOWED-OUT VERTEBRA OF A WHALE*

THE **SAN DIEGUITO RIVER** of San Pasqual, Calif., IS KNOWN AS THE *SANTA YSABEL CREEK* AT ITS SOURCE, AS THE *SAN PASQUAL* AND *BERNARDO RIVER* IN ITS COURSE, AND AS THE *SAN DIEGUITO* AT ITS MOUTH

191

THE ARCH
ERECTED IN Cleethorpes, England, ON A HOT JULY DAY IN 1885 FOR A VISIT BY PRINCE ALBERT VICTOR, GRANDSON OF QUEEN VICTORIA, WAS A REPLICA OF FAMED MARBLE ARCH —*BUT IT WAS MADE OF HUNDREDS OF TONS OF NORWEGIAN ICE*

PERCE C. SAWYER of Duck Key, Fla., LOST HIS FALSE TEETH IN HURRICANE DONNA IN 1960— AND *THEY WERE FOUND 3 MONTHS LATER* **IMBEDDED IN CORAL ROCK HALF A MILE AWAY**

BELMONT ABBEY in Belmont, N.C., IS THE ONLY CATHEDRAL ABBEY IN THE UNITED STATES — *A COMPLETE DIOCESE IN ITSELF*